◆◆◆ 本シリーズの特徴と使い方 ◆◆◆

　本シリーズでは、これからの世界において生きていく上で必要な様々な社会問題への気づきを、スクリプトの助けを借りた映像の視聴と、関連題材のリーディングを通して高めていきます。また、単に情報の受信・受容だけにとどまらず、手に入れた情報□□□□□□□自分の考えを付け加えて発信していくことを到達点として□□□□□□□□□□□□□□□良い英語学習を、段階を追って進めていくことが可能となっ□□□□□□□

　これからの社会では、「他人の靴をはく□□□□□□□□□□ne's shoes）、つまりエンパシー（empathy）を身につける□□□□□□□□□ていています。他者の行動や経験、感情を（情緒的ではなく）認知的に理解する能力のことといっても良いでしょう。エンパシーは決して生得的な資質ではなく、経験を積みながら身に付けていくものといわれていますが、この力はおいそれとは身に付きません。様々な経験を積み、考え、悩み、その中で自分の意見を形成していく過程を通してのみ、エンパシーは身に付くのです。しかし、「多様な社会で多様な経験を積み」といわれても、なかなかそのような機会が得られないのも我々の現実でしょう。

　そこで本シリーズでは、**Video Watching** のコーナーを中核に据え、ジャンクフードから菜食主義、カーボンニュートラルから伝統の継承、自動運転から字幕の翻訳、気候変動から貧困の問題、そして種の保存から動物との共生まで様々な社会的話題を、北米や欧州以外の視点も取り入れながら提示し、不足しがちな多様な経験の補助となるよう心がけました。また、考えを深め、悩み、自分の意見を形成するために、**Script Reading** では対立する意見を映像で見たり、スクリプトで読んだりできるように題材を選択しました。加えて、**Further Information** のコーナーでは異なる視点も取り入れることができるよう、様々なジャンルの比較的短い英文パッセージを提示していきます（授業時間数にあわせてご利用ください）。

　さらに、英語を学ぶために必須の、(a) インプットとアウトプットのバランス（**Video Watching, Your Opinion**）、(b) 語彙の増強と推測能力の向上（**Vocabulary Check 1st/2nd Rounds**）、(c) 全体の把握と細部の把握（**For Gist, True or False, Comprehension Check**）、そして (d) 情報の再編成（**Retelling the Story**）などにも十分に配慮し、到達目標である自分の意見の表明（**Your Opinion**）にまで、段階的に誘導するように心がけました。

　このような様々な工夫を凝らした本シリーズでの学びを通して、学習者諸氏が、バランスの良い英語力とこれからの社会を生き抜くためのエンパシーの力、そして様々な社会問題への気づきを高めて頂ければ、編著者一同、これにまさる喜びはありません。

　最後になりましたが、本シリーズの編集の労を執ってくださっている（株）松柏社の森有紀子副社長に、心より感謝したいと思います。

2023年初秋　編著者一同

i

Contents

If You Can Imagine It, Artificial Intelligence Can Create It

▶▶▶

アメリカの企業OpenAIにより開発されたDALL-E 2による画像生成技術の可能性を探ります。GAN（Generative Adversarial Network）を使い自然言語で記述されたイメージを生成するDALL-E 2。カリフォルニア大学バークレー校の教授・ハニー・ファリドさんはその技術に感心する一方で問題点も発見しています。

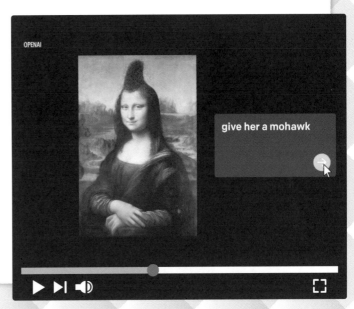

Video Watching for Gist

Watch the video and pick up five keywords. Guess what the main theme (topic/issue) of the video clip is.

Vocabulary Check – 1st Round

Match the following words and phrases with correct Japanese meanings.

1. relevant ・矛盾
2. inconsistency ・手がかり
3. clue ・〜を拡散する
4. distribute ・〜を歪める
5. distort ・関連のある

3 Video Watching & Script Reading 🔊 Audio 02

Watch the video and fill in the appropriate words in the blanks.

Reporter: From an astronaut riding a horse to a Shiba Inu dog wearing a beret, the possibilities are seemingly endless with DALL-E 2. It's the latest iteration of an Artificial Intelligence-based image generator by San Francisco tech company OpenAI. The neural network is trained on hundreds of millions of images paired with captions and can translate virtually any text prompt into a relevant image. Even seemingly random prompts: a sea otter in the style of *Girl with a Pearl Earring* by Johannes Vermeer. 19-year-old Ilan Breines is **1.**_____ **2.**_____ only a million users who have had a chance to play with DALL-E 2.

Ilan Breines: I don't think anyone thinks it's going to like replace like real artists and graphic design, but I think it'll more be like a tool for artists to like streamline their creative process.

Reporter: University of California Berkeley professor and digital forensics researcher Hany Farid has tested DALL-E 2 and is equally impressed.

2

20 **Hany Farid:** My first impression was, I was completely blown away.

Reporter: Still, Farid discovered that DALL-E 2 doesn't always 3._____ 4._____ 5._____ when it comes to perspective. Like these images produced from the prompt, "three cubes on a sidewalk photographed on 25 a sunny day."

Hany Farid: This is a complete failure, it just put the shadows in the wrong place.

Reporter: These and other inconsistencies are clues, Farid says, that can help researchers like him determine whether 30 an image is 6._____ 7._____ fake. But as systems become more advanced, it'll get harder to tell differences. Farid says the scale of the output will be a challenge to stay 8._____ 9._____ 10._____ .

35 **Hany Farid:** We're not dealing with a couple of images a week, a couple of images a year, a month, we're dealing with thousands of images every hour, that can now be synthesized and distributed and distorting reality.

Reporter: For now, DALL-E 2 is pushing the boundaries of art 40 imitating life. Tina Trinh, VOA News, New York.

📖 **Notes**

ℓ.3 **DALL-E 2** 画家のサルバドール・ダリや、ピクサーの長編アニメ映画『ウォーリー』(WALL-E) のキャラクターが名前の由来となっている。／ℓ.3 **iteration** 「(ソフトウェアなどの) バージョン・版」／ℓ.5 **OpenAI** 人工知能の開発を行なう企業。2022年11月にChatGPTを公開した。2023年12月27日、ニューヨーク・タイムズ (NYT) はOpenAIと同社に出資するマイクロソフトを、NYTの記事をAIの学習用に許可なく使用したことによる著作権侵害をしているとして提訴した。／ℓ.5 **neural network** 脳の神経細胞 (ニューロン) のネットワーク構造を模倣した数学モデル。／ℓ.6 **caption** 「(写真・図表などの) 短い説明文、キャプション」／ℓ.7 **virtually** 「事実上」／ℓ.7 **prompt** 「プロンプト」コンピュータ画面に表示して指示を促す記号やメッセージ。／ℓ.8 **sea otter** 「ラッコ」／ℓℓ.9–10 **Johannes Vermeer** 「ヨハネス・フェルメール」17世紀のオランダ黄金時代を代表する画家。／ℓ.15 **streamline** 「(業務や作業工程など) を効率化する」／ℓℓ.17–18 **digital forensic** 「デジタル・フォレンジック (電子情報の科学捜査)」forensicは法医学の意。／ℓ.20 **be blown away** 「圧倒される」／ℓ.23 **perspective** 「(絵画などの) 遠近法」／ℓ.32 **scale** 「規模」／ℓ.38 **synthesize** 「~を電子機器で合成する」／ℓ.39 **push the boundary** 「限界に挑戦する」／ℓ.40 **life** 「実物」

4 ▶ Vocabulary Check – 2nd Round ···················

Choose the appropriate words below to fill in the blanks in the English sentences. Change forms if necessary.

| deal with | determine | fake | imitate | when it comes to |

1. Investigators are still trying to _____ the cause of the fire.

2. _____ computer programming, nobody can beat him.

3. The president has flown home to _____ the crisis caused by the hurricane.

4. He has a unique ability to _____ any sound he has heard.

5. The man was arrested when entering the country with a _____ passport.

5 ▶ True or False ··································

Read the following statements and indicate whether they are true (T) or not (F) along with the reasons. If you cannot determine T or F from the text, indicate NG (not given).

1. DALL-E 2 is an art-generating software developed by a company called OpenAI.   **(T / F / NG)**

_____

2. Some artists have made use of DALL-E 2 to generate ideas.   **(T / F / NG)**

_____

3. Professor Farid was not really surprised by DALL-E 2's ability to create images.   **(T / F / NG)**

_____

Comprehension Check ·······················

Choose the best answer for each question.

1. Why can DALL-E 2 create images?

   a. because it studies features of images by individual artists

   b. because it studies texts translated by artists to match images

   c. because it studies both the images and explanations about them

2. How did Professor Farid find out that the image created from the prompt, "three cubes on a sidewalk photographed on a sunny day" was fake?

   a. by measuring the perspective ratio

   b. by checking the direction of shadows

   c. by comparing the images with real objects

3. Why is identifying fake images challenging?

   a. because a large number of fake images spread so quickly

   b. because the number of digital forensic experts is small

   c. because many companies are developing similar software

 Retelling the Story ·······························

Re-tell the story presented in the video clip, including the following five keywords.

| an image generator | artificial intelligence | real artists |
| fake images | tell the difference between |

DALLE-2 is an image generator that uses artificial intelligence technology to create images. With

a few prompts, it can generate images like ones created by real artists. Although there are errors

in AI-generated images, it is easy to create fake images. As the technology advances, it will become

harder to tell the difference between fake and real images.

Your Opinion in Writing ·······················

Would you call AI-generated images "art"? Write your opinion in at least six sentences.

I don't think we can call AI-generated images "art". It's fun to play with image-generating software like DALL-E2, and everyone can enjoy this technology. However, AI creates images by putting together pieces of existing art. There is no thought. Real art is created by artists with years of experience, effort, thought, love and passion. We should draw a line between the products of AI and the work of artists. No matter how much technology advances, I don't think AI can replace real artists.

9 **Further Information** ····························· Audio 03

Read below.

OpenAI   Research ⌄   Product ⌄   Development ⌄   Safety ⌄   Company ⌄   Search

A focus on safety

DALL·E 2 began as a research project and is now available in beta[*1]. Safety mitigations[*2] we have developed and continue to improve upon include:

Preventing harmful generations

We've limited the ability for DALL·E 2 to generate violent, hate, or adult images. By removing the most explicit content from the training data, we minimized DALL·E 2's exposure to these concepts. We also used advanced techniques to prevent photorealistic generations of real individuals' faces, including those of public figures.

 Notes

[*1] **beta** 「ベータ版（β版）」正式版のリリース前にユーザーに試用してもらうためのサンプルのソフトウェア。 [*2] **safety (risk) mitigation** 「安全リスク緩和」

Cooking Show Re-Creates Age-Old Recipes

▶▶▶

マックス・ミラーのYouTubeチャンネル「Tasting History」。思いがけない理由で始めたチャンネルですが、登録者数は100万人を超えました。ローマ時代後期や4千年前のバビロニア王国のレシピを作って見せる彼の食を通した歴史探究の冒険を共有してみましょう！

1 Video Watching for Gist

Watch the video and pick up five keywords. Guess what the main theme (topic/issue) of the video clip is.

2 Vocabulary Check – 1st Round

Match the following words and phrases with correct Japanese meanings.

1. fermented	・〜を一時解雇する
2. mussel	・料理の
3. donation	・発酵させた
4. furlough	・寄付金
5. culinary	・ムール貝

Video Watching & Script Reading 🔊 Audio 04

Watch the video and fill in the appropriate words in the blanks.

Reporter: Exploring ancient recipes and testing them in his kitchen. One of Max Miller's favorites uses caraway seeds, fermented fish sauce and other ingredients to recreate Parthian chicken, a Persian dish from people
5 who lived on the edge of the Roman world. Or mussels prepared, according to a recipe from a late Roman era cookbook.

Max Miller: After about 5 minutes, 1.＿＿＿＿＿＿ 2.＿＿＿＿＿＿ 3.＿＿＿＿＿＿ and if most of the mussels have opened,
10 you're 4.＿＿＿＿＿＿ 5.＿＿＿＿＿＿ go.

Reporter: Miller's YouTube channel, Tasting History, has more than 1 million subscribers. Producing episodes is his full-time job, financed by YouTube advertising, donations from viewers and commercial sponsorships. Miller used
15 to work in marketing and distribution at Walt Disney Pictures, but was furloughed when COVID hit and his hobby, a cooking channel, became his job.

Max Miller: Then I had plenty of time because I had nothing to do.

Reporter: Pastries from ancient to recent times. If he can find
20 the recipe, he's willing to try it. This 4000-year-old

Babylonian recipe for lamb and beef stew produces a dish surprisingly like traditional Slavic borscht.

Max Miller: And it's just interesting to see how these dishes, if they're good, persist throughout time.

25 Reporter: Other dishes are less 6._____ 7._____ liking, like a stew of pork and blood from ancient Greece.

Max Miller: And here we are. Melas Zomos, Spartan black broth.

Reporter: Exploring history through food. The good and the bad.

Max Miller: Food and history, and, you know, I don't have a budget
30 of any kind. I just sit at my kitchen counter and my too-small-to-even-film-in kitchen, and... I did not think anybody 8._____ 9._____ 10._____ . But they are.

Reporter: With hundreds of thousands of viewers joining his
35 culinary adventures. Mike O'Sullivan, VOA News, Los Angeles.

📖 **Notes**

ℓℓ.2–3 **caraway seeds**「キャラウェイの実」香辛料の一種。爽快感があり、甘い香りとほろ苦い味が特徴。／ℓ.4 **Parthian**「パルティア風」パルティアはペルシャ帝国の一王朝であるアルサケス朝を指す。BC250～AD230頃に、現在のイランを中心に存在。／ℓ.4 **Persian**「ペルシャ風」ペルシャ帝国の一時代の古代ペルシャ王朝はBC550～AD330頃に存在。／ℓ.5 **Roman**「ローマ帝国の」ローマ帝国はBC30～AD1450頃に存在。／ℓ.21 **Babylonian**「バビロニア王国の」イラク、メソポタミア南部、チグリス・ユーフラテス川下流地方の古名。／ℓ.22 **Slavic**「スラブ民族の」スラブ民族はヨーロッパ東部から中部にかけて居住する。／ℓ.22 **borscht**「ボルシチ」牛肉をビーツ、玉葱、人参などの野菜で煮込んだスープで、ウクライナ伝承の家庭料理。／ℓ.27 **Melas Zomos**「メラス・ゾーモス」古代ギリシャのスパルタにて食された料理で、豚の足と血、塩、酢を混ぜ合わせて作られた黒いスープ。／ℓ.27 **Spartan**「スパルタの」スパルタは古代ギリシャの都市国家。／ℓ.27 **broth**「(肉・野菜・米・魚などの)スープ」／ℓ.31 **too-small-to-even-film**「狭すぎて(映画の)撮影もできない」

4 ▶ Vocabulary Check – 2nd Round

Choose the appropriate words below to fill in the blanks in the English sentences. Change forms if necessary.

ancient	budget	ingredient	lamb	persist

1. Choosing either sirloin steak or leg of _____ is difficult in this restaurant.

2. If the pain _____ after 24 hours, consult your doctor.

3. In Rome, you can visit many _____ monuments.

4. Many university students have to live within a tight _____.

5. Mix all the _____ together in a large bowl.

5 ▶ True or False

Read the following statements and indicate whether they are true (T) or not (F) along with the reasons. If you cannot determine T or F from the text, indicate NG (not given).

1. Max Miller started his cooking YouTube channel to promote himself as a chef.

(T / F / NG)

_____

2. Miller is attracted by how ancient recipes survived in history.   (T / F / NG)

_____

3. He now has enough budget to visit foreign countries and explore their foods.

(T / F / NG)

_____

Comprehension Check ··

Choose the best answer for each question.

1. What ingredients does Miller use for his favorite recipe of the Roman era?

    a. chicken

    b. fish

    c. lamb

2. Why did Miller start his YouTube channel during COVID?

    a. because he had plenty of time to spend

    b. because he had to earn more money

    c. because he wanted to be connected with people online

3. What sort of recipes is he interested in trying?

    a. anything he can find

    b. ones that his subscribers request him to cook

    c. only those he wants to serve to his friends

 Retelling the Story ··

Re-tell the story presented in the video clip, including the following five keywords.

| COVID | ancient recipes | YouTube channel | subscribers |

| full-time job |

8 **Your Opinion in Writing** ···

If you would start a new YouTube channel related to your hobby, what kind of channel would you like to do? Why?

_____

_____

_____

_____

_____

 9 **Further Information** ································· 🔊 **Audio 05**

Read the passage below.

"Ekiben" Station Lunchboxes Taking Root[*1] in Paris, the City of Haute Cuisine[*2] ?

© Hanazen

Travelers decide on their ekiben with explanations from French staff. President Yagihashi looks on in his *happi*. © Hanazen

Ekiben, "station lunchboxes," are a staple of Japan's train riding culture. In November 2021, the Akita Prefecture *ekiben* specialist Hanazen[*3] opened a shop in Paris's Gare de Lyon[*4] station—the first time one of Japan's *ekiben* shops has opened in a European station.

Japanese cuisine, or *washoku*, has garnered worldwide attention since its 2013 UNESCO Intangible Heritage listing[*5]. Bento, a popular Japanese-run lunch box specialist, now has around 70 locations in Paris, but only the most clued-in[*6] Japan fan is aware

5 of the world of *ekiben*. Now, though, all 200 ekiben prepared for the day at Gare de Lyon sell out by 5:00 pm. "France might be at the bleeding edge[*7] of fashion, with the Paris Collection and all, but it still respects older culture. It's fertile soil for *ekiben* culture to take root," says Hanazen President Yagihashi Shūichi, who took

10 it upon himself to[*8] go out and attract customers.

One thing the firm discovered was that French customers preferred the flavored *takikomi-gohan* to white rice. "For most overseas diners, not just French people, sushi is the gateway to Japanese cuisine, which means they eat the rice with soy sauce.

15 So, from that perspective, the rice in our *torimeshi* is already flavored with soy sauce and sugar. People actually complimented us on our great idea, since they didn't have to add any soy sauce."

Customers buying the Akita bentō also get a bookmark
made by Ōdate elementary school students. © Hanazen

 Notes

[*1] **take root** 「根付く」／ [*2] **haute cuisine** 《仏語》「高級料理」／ [*3] **Hanazen** 「花善」秋田を代表する鶏めし弁当を販売している会社。／ [*4] **Gare de Lyon** 「リヨン駅」Gareはフランス語で「駅」の意味。／ [*5] **UNESCO Intangible Heritage listing** 「ユネスコ無形文化遺産登録」／ [*6] **clued-in** 「～に詳しい、精通している」／ [*7] **bleeding edge** 「最先端」／ [*8] **take it upon oneself to ~** 「～する役目を自ら引き受ける」

Vocabulary Checklist

Check the boxes after reviewing the meanings
of the words listed below.

Unit 1
If You Can Imagine It,
Artificial Intelligence Can Create It

☐ relevant   ☐ fake

☐ be blown away   ☐ determine

☐ when it comes to   ☐ distribute

☐ inconsistency   ☐ distort

☐ clue   ☐ imitate

Unit 2
Cooking Show Re-Creates
Age-Old Recipes

☐ ancient   ☐ furlough

☐ fermented   ☐ lamb

☐ ingredient   ☐ persist

☐ mussel   ☐ budget

☐ donation   ☐ culinary

Los Angeles Airport Finds Success with Therapy Dogs to Unstress Passengers

動物保護活動家のヒュブナーさんは2013年、ペットによる飛行機の乗客のストレス解消プログラムを開始。数百人のボランティアと犬たちが何千人もの乗客の気持ちを穏やかにしてきました。セラピー犬となる唯一無二の条件は、犬も人も誰もが楽しめる環境です。

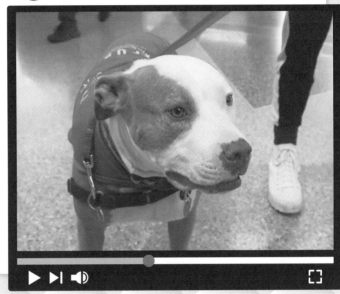

 ## Video Watching for Gist

Watch the video and pick up five keywords. Guess what the main theme (topic/issue) of the video clip is.

2 Vocabulary Check – 1st Round

Match the following words and phrases with correct Japanese meanings.

1. foundation	・	不機嫌な
2. moody	・	設立
3. entertainment	・	安らぎ
4. temptation	・	楽しみ
5. comfort	・	誘惑

3 Video Watching & Script Reading 🔊 Audio 06

Watch the video and fill in the appropriate words in the blanks.

Reporter:	These dogs are not at the Los Angeles International Airport to hop on a plane. They work here. Sergio, Klaus and Monte are therapy dogs here at the airport.
Reporter:	Animal lover and rescuer Heidi Huebner started the Pets Unstressing Passengers program in 2013 to help people feeling anxious at airports. In the nine years since its foundation, **1.**_____ **2.**_____ **3.**_____ and dogs have made thousands of passengers feel calmer.
Heidi Huebner:	You just don't really know what to expect when you're coming to travel. So when we have the therapy dogs here it's just that warm and friendly, like, Oh, I can breathe and just feel happy.
Reporter:	Passengers love this innovation.

5

10

Tara:	Oh, it's such a good idea, because we're like on the plane and tired and moody and then we **4.**_____ **5.**_____ and get to see dogs. I love dogs. It always makes me happy, so I definitely believe into that. Yeah.
Michelle:	The few of us that get delayed flights, any entertainment is wonderful. And, you know, pets make everybody smile.

15

20

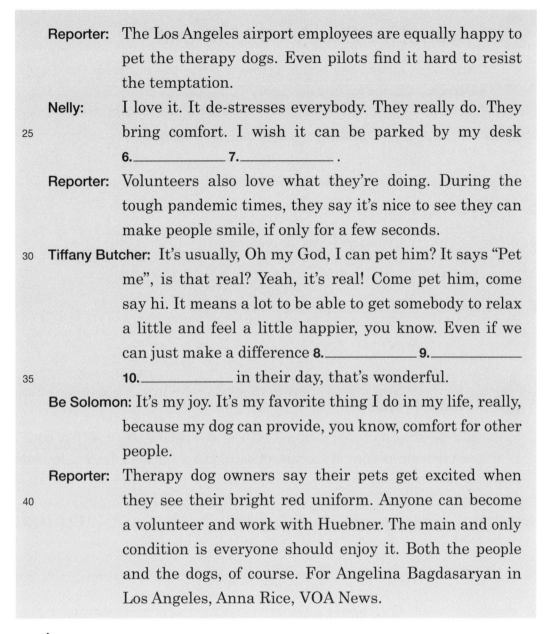

Reporter: The Los Angeles airport employees are equally happy to pet the therapy dogs. Even pilots find it hard to resist the temptation.

Nelly: I love it. It de-stresses everybody. They really do. They
25 bring comfort. I wish it can be parked by my desk 6._____ 7._____ .

Reporter: Volunteers also love what they're doing. During the tough pandemic times, they say it's nice to see they can make people smile, if only for a few seconds.

30 **Tiffany Butcher:** It's usually, Oh my God, I can pet him? It says "Pet me", is that real? Yeah, it's real! Come pet him, come say hi. It means a lot to be able to get somebody to relax a little and feel a little happier, you know. Even if we can just make a difference 8._____ 9._____
35 10._____ in their day, that's wonderful.

Be Solomon: It's my joy. It's my favorite thing I do in my life, really, because my dog can provide, you know, comfort for other people.

Reporter: Therapy dog owners say their pets get excited when
40 they see their bright red uniform. Anyone can become a volunteer and work with Huebner. The main and only condition is everyone should enjoy it. Both the people and the dogs, of course. For Angelina Bagdasaryan in Los Angeles, Anna Rice, VOA News.

Notes

ℓℓ.2–3 **Sergio, Klaus and Monte** 犬の名前／ℓ.5 **unstressing**「ストレスをなくすこと」／ℓ.13 **breathe**「ひと息入れる」／ℓ.22 **resist**「抵抗する」／ℓ.24 **de-stress**「ストレスを解消する」／ℓ.28 **pandemic**「疾病の世界的大流行」 ここでは新型コロナ感染症のことを指す。／ℓ.30 **pet**〔動詞〕「かわいがる」／ℓ.34 **make a difference**「（状況を）良くする」

Vocabulary Check – 2nd Round ·····················

Choose the appropriate words below to fill in the blanks in the English sentences. Change forms if necessary.

expect	anxious	resist	innovation	delay

1. I always feel _____ before the presentation.

2. It was unfortunate that her flight _____ .

3. I _____ the package to arrive tomorrow.

4. The company is known for its constant _____ its technology.

5. He managed to _____ eating the entire cake.

5 **True or False** ··································

Read the following statements and indicate whether they are true (T) or not (F) along with the reasons. If you cannot determine T or F from the text, indicate NG (not given).

1. Only a few people can work with therapy dogs.　　　　**(T / F / NG)**

_____

2. Passengers at the Los Angeles International Airport appreciate therapy dogs.

(T / F / NG)

_____

3. Employees and pilots are allowed to feed therapy dogs.　**(T / F / NG)**

_____

6 Comprehension Check ·····································

Choose the best answer for each question.

1. What is the purpose of the Pets Unstressing Passengers program?

   a. to train dogs for airplane travel

   b. to help anxious travellers at airports

   c. to rescue people in emergent situation

2. What do volunteers say about therapy dogs during the tough pandemic times?

   a. The dogs also tend to feel stressed as people do.

   b. The dogs can make people smile.

   c. The program hasn't been running during the pandemic.

3. Why do the therapy dogs get excited to see their bright red uniforms?

   a. because they are excited to see their owners at the airport

   b. because they are participating in a special event at the airport

   c. because they are ready to provide comfort for people at the airport

7 Retelling the Story ·····································

Re-tell the story presented in the video clip, including the following five keywords.

| assist travelers | therapy dogs | airport employees | feel happy |

| provide comfort |

_____

_____

8 Your Opinion in Writing ·····································

Do you think therapy dogs can work well in more public facilities? Write your opinion in at least six sentences.

_____

_____

_____

_____

_____

_____

9 **Further Information** ·········· Audio 07

Read the passage below.

About the International Therapy Dog Association

WHAT WE DO

At the International Therapy Dog Association (ITDA), based on
the principle of animal welfare, we rescue dogs before they are
put down*1 at the dog pounds*2 or shelters. These may be strays*3

5 or other dogs that have no owners for
various reasons, such as due to the 2011
earthquake and tsunami. We take them
in, train them as therapy dogs, and by
doing so try to realize a society*4 where

10 there is "zero culling*5". These dogs start
their new life as therapy dogs, and by
making social contributions, we hope to
achieve a society where dogs and humans
can coexist*6.

© International Therapy Dog Association

Rescued strays and dogs from the disaster area. Therapy dogs bring courage and hope to many people. Founder Toru Oki (left) and therapy dog Chirori (center). © International Therapy Dog Association

---

 Notes

*1 **put down**「（動物を）殺処分する、安楽死させる」／ *2 **dog pound**「犬の保護施設」／ *3 **stray**
「野良犬」／ *4 **by doing so try to realize a society** try toの前にweを補うと文章を把握しやすい。
／ *5 **culling** [kʌlɪŋ]「殺処分」／ *6 **coexist**「共存する」

Vocabulary Checklist

Check the boxes after reviewing the meanings
of the words listed below.

Unit 3
Los Angeles Airport Finds Success
with Therapy Dogs to Unstress Passengers

☐ anxious   ☐ delayed

☐ foundation   ☐ entertainment

☐ expect   ☐ resist

☐ innovation   ☐ temptation

☐ moody   ☐ comfort

For Generation Z, It's Travel Now, Work Later

▶▶▶

コロナ禍以降、出社が前提だった人々の働き方はリモートワークを含むものに変わってきています。その結果、ミレニアム世代やX世代とZ世代とでは、仕事に対する考え方が異なってきているといいます。それはつまり、人生において重視することが、世代により異なってきたことを意味するようです。ワークライフバランスを重視し、自分自身を大切にすることについて考えてみましょう。

 ## Video Watching for Gist

Watch the video and pick up five keywords. Guess what the main theme (topic/issue) of the video clip is.

 ## Vocabulary Check – 1st Round

Match the following words and phrases with correct Japanese meanings.

1. perspective	・〜が気になる
2. sign up	・映画撮影技術（法）
3. cinematography	・視点
4. care about	・忠誠心
5. loyalty	・労働契約を結ぶ

Watch the video and fill in the appropriate words in the blanks.

Reporter: Isabelle Liebling is 23, making her one of the older members of Generation Z, or Zoomers, as they're known. In 2021, **1.**_____ **2.**_____ a student, she spent all her savings on a trip to Europe. But she doesn't
5 regret it. And today, talking to her thousands of followers on TikTok, she encourages young people to do the same.

Isabelle Liebling: I'll make the money back, but I'll never be in my twenties again traveling.

Reporter: Liebling recently graduated from university and now
10 works **3.**_____ **4.**_____ IT engineer. But her main priority is traveling, not building a career.

Isabelle Liebling: Traveling, seeing 19 different countries in Europe, changed my perspective again. I had signed up, I was going to be in a job where I'd be going in every day, lots
15 of hours, and I decided to change that. I quit that job with one that allows for more of a work life balance, and hopefully remote.

Reporter: 20-year-old student Cameron Wade hopes to combine travel and work as well. A cinematography student
20 at Michigan University, she believes the Internet has changed the traditional show-up-to-the-office-to-work way of doing business.

Cameron Wade: The Internet is a really big aspect in our generation. It's like we have a way to reach a broad amount of people,
25 even from our own homes.

Reporter: The Zoomers who we spoke to say they care about taking care of themselves and finding a way to combine the important aspects of their lives.

Isabelle Liebling: At least for my parents, with that first job I hated,

30   they were like, Stick with it. Pull yourself up by your bootstraps. Maybe in three years you'll get what you want. In our generation, we don't want to waste our time, 5.＿＿＿＿＿ 6.＿＿＿＿＿ 7.＿＿＿＿＿ loyalty to one company that's no longer serving us.

35 **Reporter:** According to Pew Research Center, Zoomers belong to the most educated generation in history, with some 57% attending a university or college. Only 52% of millennials and 43% of Generation Xers chose higher education. Sociologists agree that just because young

40   people want a nontraditional work experience, doesn't mean they 8.＿＿＿＿＿ 9.＿＿＿＿＿ 10.＿＿＿＿＿ productive. Experiences during their youth could help them long-term, experts say.

 Cassie Holmes: Research shows that people investing in experiences

45   leads to greater happiness than previous generations spending more on material goods. And the research shows that not only does it have an initial effect where experiential purchases lead to greater happiness, but that effect is longer lasting.

50 **Reporter:** Experts say that by 2025 generation Z workers will make up over a quarter of the U.S. workforce. Karina Bafradzhian, VOA News, Washington.

📖✏️ **Notes**

***Title* Generation Z**「Z世代」1990年代中頃～2010年代初め頃に生まれた世代。生まれた時点でインターネットが利用可能であった世代。／ *ℓℓ*.**18–19 combine A and B**「AとBを両立させる」／ *ℓ*.**20 the Internet**「インターネット」冒頭に必ずtheが付き、大文字で始まることに注意。／ *ℓℓ*.**21–22 show-up-to-the-office-to-work way**「出社して仕事をするやり方」／ *ℓ*.**23 aspect**「要素、特徴」／ *ℓ*.**26 zoomer**「Z世代の人」／ *ℓℓ*.**30–31 pull oneself up by one's bootstraps**「自力で困難を乗り越える」／ *ℓ*.**38 millennial**「ミレニアル世代」1980年頃～1990年代半ば頃に生まれ、2000年以降に成人になった世代。10代からデジタル環境になじんだ初の世代に当たる。／ *ℓ*.**38 Generation Xer** 1965～81年頃に生まれた世代のことで、Z世代の子どもを持つ世代とも言われている。

4 ▶ Vocabulary Check – 2nd Round ······················

Choose the appropriate words below to fill in the blanks in the English sentences. Change forms if necessary.

aspect	invest	priority	regret	savings

1. Traveling abroad exposes you to cultural _____ .

2. She will _____ not taking the advice given to her.

3. I plan to _____ some money in the stock market.

4. She used her _____ to buy a new laptop for college.

5. The safety of students is the school's highest _____ .

5 ▶ True or False ·································

Read the following statements and indicate whether they are true (T) or not (F) along with the reasons. If you cannot determine T or F from the text, indicate NG (not given).

1. Zoomers want to avoid devoting most of their time to work. **(T / F / NG)**

_____

2. Compared to millennials and Generation Xers, a higher percentage of Zoomers receive more education. **(T / F / NG)**

_____

3. According to research, happiness brought by experiences is bigger than that brought by material goods, and lasts for a short time. **(T / F / NG)**

_____

Comprehension Check ································

Choose the best answer for each question.

1. What kind of job did Isabelle Liebling choose?

    a. a job where she would be going in every day

    b. a job that she can devote lots of hours to

    c. a job in which she can enjoy her private life

2. What does Cameron Wade want to focus on in her job?

    a. meeting people face to face to learn new perspectives

    b. reaching people in extended areas using the Internet

    c. working individually as much as possible

3. What did Liebling's parents think about her first job?

    a. It is better for her to change it within three years.

    b. She should not quit it so soon.

    c. People usually cannot feel loyalty to it at first.

Retelling the Story ································

Re-tell the story presented in the video clip, including the following five keywords.

Zoomers	private	experiences	material goods	happier

_____

_____

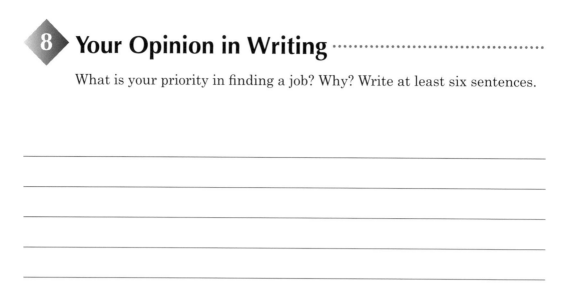

◆8 ▶ Your Opinion in Writing ·······································

What is your priority in finding a job? Why? Write at least six sentences.

_____

_____

_____

_____

_____

_____

Further Information ···································· 🔊 **Audio 09**

Read the passage below.

Time use of millennials and Generation X: differences across time

The table below presents the average hours per day millennials[1] in 2019 and members of Generation X in 2003 spent on various activities, the percentage of people in each generation who did the activities on a given day[2], and the average durations of the activities for those who did them
5 on a given day.

Table▼Time spent in various activities and percent of the Generation X (2003) and millennial (2019) populations, ages 23 to 38, engaging in each activity.

Activity	Average hours per day, civilian population		Average percentage engaged in the activity per day	
	Generation X (2003)	Millennials (2019)	Generation X (2003)	Millennials (2019)
Total, all activities	24.00	24.00	100.0	100.0
Eating and drinking	1.16	1.12	90.9	95.9
Household activities[3]	1.65	1.58	71.8	78.2
Food preparation and cleanup	0.52	0.62	51.1	62.0
Animals and pets	0.07	0.11	9.6	16.6
Caring for and helping household children[4]	0.94	0.84	42.2	36.7
Relaxing and thinking	0.22	0.24	21.2	16.5
Playing games	0.12	0.29	5.9	12.5

 Notes

[1] **The table below presents the average hours per day millennials** per day と millennials の間に関係代名詞 that が省略されていることに注意。／[2] **a given day** 「ある日」／
[3] **household activities** 「家事」／[4] **household children** 「家にいる子供たち」

Vocabulary Checklist

Check the boxes after reviewing the meanings
of the words listed below.

Unit 4
For Generation Z, It's Travel Now, Work Later

☐ saving   ☐ cinematography

☐ regret   ☐ aspect

☐ priority   ☐ care about

☐ perspective   ☐ loyalty

☐ sign up   ☐ invest

The Future of Chicken May Be Grown in a Lab

▶▶▶

大豆ミートをはじめとする代替肉は皆さんにとって少しずつ身近なものになってきているのではないでしょうか。この章の動画に登場するサーモンや鶏肉はホンモノに見えますか？　この代替魚・肉の大きな利点とは何でしょうか。この細胞由来製品は一般に受け入れられるでしょうか。

 ## 1 Video Watching for Gist

Watch the video and pick up five keywords. Guess what the main theme (topic/issue) of the video clip is.

 ## 2 Vocabulary Check – 1st Round

Match the following words and phrases with correct Japanese meanings.

1. cultivate	・〜を補う
2. supplement	・代替の
3. alternative	・〜を認める
4. feasible	・（植物や農作物を）育てる
5. acknowledge	・実現可能な

3 ▸ Video Watching & Script Reading 🔊 Audio 10

Watch the video and fill in the appropriate words in the blanks.

Reporter: This picture-perfect salmon could have come from the wild or from a fish farm, but it was grown from a handful of salmon cells and cultivated in a lab at Wild Type headquarters in Northern California.

5 Justin Kolbeck: We've come up with 1._____ 2._____ 3._____ make salmon cells, and we combine that with a plant base—it's called a scaffold—which helps to give the cells the right structure to some of the cuts that you're familiar with.

10 Reporter: As the world demand for fish and meat increases, some companies are trying to find novel ways to supplement existing supplies.

Justin Kolbeck: So our idea was, let's give them another option that doesn't involve putting added pressure on wild fisheries 15 or continuing to rely on farmed fish.

Reporter: Meanwhile, at nearby UPSIDE Foods 4._____ 5._____ were underway for these chicken bites, which were cultivated from chicken cells. They look and apparently taste just as chicken should.

20 Diner: Wow. That is chicken.

Amy Chen: It's real meat that's grown directly from animal cells, so you don't 6._____ 7._____ raise or slaughter animals.

Reporter: Ricardo San Martin, who runs the Alternative Meats 25 Lab at UC Berkeley, says bringing cell-based products to the mass market may not be realistic anytime soon.

Ricardo San Martin: Scaling up just cells to produce meat, that's not feasible. We need to know how affordable this will be. You know, is this going to be a solution for everyone or

30   just an elite?

Reporter: Alternative meat companies acknowledge that their concept is still a work in progress.

Justin Kolbeck: Let's make that first great product that can show what's possible with this technology, and then let's figure

35   out every possible way to scale this up and 8._____ 9._____ 10._____ affordable and accessible as possible.

Reporter: It's progress that is moving slowly but could one day change how the world eats. Julie Taboh, VOA News.

📖✏️ **Notes**

*ℓ.*2 **fish farm**「養魚場」farmは動詞で「（家畜を）飼育する、（魚を）養殖する」という意味になることもある。／ *ℓ.*3–4 **Wild Type** サンフランシスコに拠点を置く、細胞培養の会社。／ *ℓ.*4 **headquarters**「本社」複数形で使うことに注意。／ *ℓ.*7 **plant base**「植物性の下地」／ *ℓ.*11 **novel**「斬新な、画期的な」／ *ℓ.*14 **fishery**「漁場」／ *ℓ.*16 **UPSIDE Foods** バークレーに拠点を置く人工培養肉製造のベンチャー企業。2022年11月、アメリカ食品医薬品局（FDA）から培養鶏肉の安全性を世界で初めて認められた。／ *ℓ.*17 **chicken bites**「一口サイズのチキン料理」biteは食べ物の一口分。／ *ℓ.*23 **slaughter**「～を畜殺（食肉処理）する」／ *ℓ.*25 **UC Berkeley**「カリフォルニア大学バークレー校」／ *ℓ.*30 **elite**「上流階級」

4 ▶ Vocabulary Check – 2nd Round ···················

Choose the appropriate words below to fill in the blanks in the English sentences. Change forms if necessary.

| affordable | cell | come up with | figure out | underway |

1. An investigation is _____ to discover the cause of last night's train crash.

2. It took me three days to _____ what was wrong with my computer.

3. Nowadays, there are many treatments which destroy cancer _____.

4. How did you _____ such a crazy idea?

5. There is a shortage of _____ housing in the urban area.

5 ▶ True or False ································

Read the following statements and indicate whether they are true (T) or not (F) along with the reasons. If you cannot determine T or F from the text, indicate NG (not given).

1. One of the reasons for developing cell-based salmon at Wild Type is to support the declining number of fishermen. **(T / F / NG)**

_____

2. Chicken bites made from chicken cells are as good as real chicken.

(T / F / NG)

_____

3. Alternative meat grown from cells has been increasing on the market.

(T / F / NG)

_____

Comprehension Check ··

Choose the best answer for each question.

1. Why is a plant base added to make cell-based salmon at the Wild Type lab?

   a. to make it taste like real salmon

   b. to create a structure similar to salmon

   c. to increase the volume of the salmon

2. What is the reason for producing alternative fish or meat?

   a. More and more people are trying to protect the wildlife.

   b. The supply of fish and meat cannot keep up with the demand.

   c. The popularity of alternative meat and fish is expected to grow.

3. How can alternative meat products be accepted by the public?

   a. by reducing prices

   b. by increasing food safety

   c. by securing enough supply

 Retelling the Story ··································

Re-tell the story presented in the video clip, including the following five keywords.

| demand for fish and meat | cell-based products | raise or kill animals |

| supply | affordable |

8 ▶ Your Opinion in Writing ·······································

Do you think cell-based products could be a solution to meet the growing demand for fish and meat? Write your opinion in at least six sentences.

---

9 ▶ Further Information ·································· 🔊 Audio 11

Read the passage below.

Meat Alternatives Making Rapid Inroads*¹ in Japan

Japan lags behind Europe and North America in*²
embracing*³ plant-based meat alternatives, but this trend has
shifted dramatically since 2020, which some industry insiders
are calling "year one" of the meat alternative era.

Soy MOS Burger (¥460)

MOS Burger's Soy MOS Burger
© Saitō Hayato

5　Major Japanese fast-food chain MOS Burger's Soy MOS
Burger is based on the company's flagship*⁴ beef product. I
tasted this one alongside the original as well, and it has all
of the meat version's rich umami flavor. The texture*⁵ and
appearance are nearly identical to*⁶ the original MOS Burger,
10　and the only difference I could detect*⁷ was that the aftertaste
seemed lighter. They are now available at branches*⁸ all over
Japan for ¥460. I highly recommend it for those wanting to try
a meat alternative product for a reasonable price.

※モスバーガーの商品についての情報は2023年10月時点のものです。

Notes

*¹ **make inroads** 「（企業が市場に）参入する」／ *² **lag behind ... in ~** 「～において…に後れをとる」
／ *³ **embrace** 「～を受け入れる」／ *⁴ **flagship** 「主力の」／ *⁵ **texture** 「食感」／ *⁶ **identical to ...**
「…とまったく同じ」／ *⁷ **detect** 「～に気づく」／ *⁸ **branch** 「店舗」

Vocabulary Checklist

Check the boxes after reviewing the meanings
of the words listed below.

Unit 5
The Future of Chicken May Be Grown in a Lab

- ☐ cell
- ☐ cultivate
- ☐ come up with
- ☐ supplement
- ☐ underway (adj.)

- ☐ alternative
- ☐ feasible
- ☐ affordable
- ☐ acknowledge
- ☐ figure out

Exhibition Explores Vibrant History of Black Filmmaking

▶ ▶ ▶

2021年9月にオープンしたアカデミー映画博物館では、アフリカ系アメリカ人の映画製作者たちの歴史にスポットを当てたブラックシネマ特集企画が開催されています。そこでは、ブラックシネマが制作されることになった歴史的背景が学べます。映画産業の一翼を担ってきた黒人エンターテナーたちの歴史を見てみましょう。

1 Video Watching for Gist

Watch the video and pick up five keywords. Guess what the main theme (topic/issue) of the video clip is.

2 Vocabulary Check – 1st Round

Match the following words and phrases with correct Japanese meanings.

1. comprehensive	・主要上映作品
2. feature films	・堂々とした
3. robust	・総合的な
4. showcase	・盛んな
5. imposing	・〜を展示する

3 Video Watching & Script Reading

Watch the video and fill in the appropriate words in the blanks.

Reporter: A classic film clip from 1898 shows a black couple kissing. Rediscovered just five years ago, it's shown with other early film clips, part of the exhibition, *Regeneration Black Cinema 1898 to 1971* at the Academy Museum of Motion Pictures, a comprehensive film museum that opened last year. And this exhibition tells an important story, say museum officials.

Jacqueline Stewart: We really wanted to take the time and the space to show people just how long black artists **1.**_____ **2.**_____ involved in filmmaking.

Reporter: Looking at black entertainers and filmmakers who faced discrimination in Hollywood, but were part of a major alternative industry that produced...

Rhea Combs: Independent film productions, primarily for an African-American audience, in large part by African-American filmmakers.

Reporter: On display are scripts from early films. Costumes from *Stormy Weather*, the 1943 musical with Lena Horne, and *Porgy and Bess* from 1959 starring Sammy Davis Jr, and poster after poster of feature films.

Rhea Combs: And many of them have been **3.**_____ **4.**_____ time, but we have these posters as wonderful reminders of this really robust period of film production.

Reporter: Most films were **5.**_____ **6.**_____ a low budget in many different genres.

Doris Berger: We have cowboy films, we have adventure films, we have dramas...

Reporter: Including the 1939 Film *Reform School* with Louise

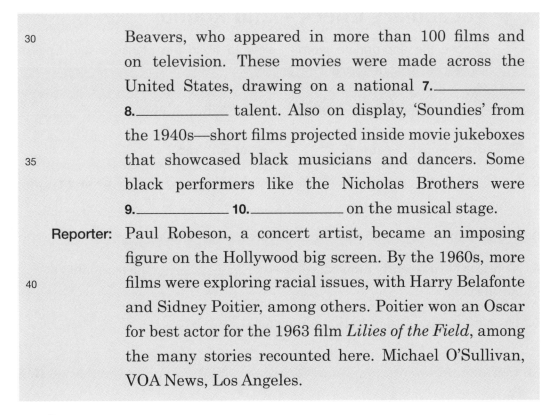

30 Beavers, who appeared in more than 100 films and on television. These movies were made across the United States, drawing on a national **7.**_____ **8.**_____ talent. Also on display, 'Soundies' from the 1940s—short films projected inside movie jukeboxes 35 that showcased black musicians and dancers. Some black performers like the Nicholas Brothers were **9.**_____ **10.**_____ on the musical stage.

Reporter: Paul Robeson, a concert artist, became an imposing figure on the Hollywood big screen. By the 1960s, more 40 films were exploring racial issues, with Harry Belafonte and Sidney Poitier, among others. Poitier won an Oscar for best actor for the 1963 film *Lilies of the Field*, among the many stories recounted here. Michael O'Sullivan, VOA News, Los Angeles.

Notes

*ℓ.*3 regeneration「再生」／*ℓ.*5 motion picture〈主に米〉「映画」／*ℓ.*6 last year ＝2021 年／*ℓ.*17 On display are scripts「展示されているのはスクリプトだ」On displayを強調した倒 置表現。／*ℓ.*18 *Stormy Weather* アフリカ系アメリカ人キャストによるハリウッドミュージカル映画と しては *Cabin in the Sky*（1943）と共に著名な作品。／*ℓ.*18 Lena Horne 米国のジャズ歌手、俳 優（1917-2010）。ブロードウェイ・ミュージカルでも舞台に立つなどしている。／*ℓ.*19 *Porgy and Bess* アメリカの作曲家ジョージ・ガーシュウィンが1935年に作曲したオペラ。ミュージカルの先駆的 な存在。／*ℓ.*19 star「（演劇や映画で）主役を演じる」／*ℓℓ.*19–20 Sammy Davis Jr（1925- 90）当時人気絶頂だったフランク・シナトラに見出された。／*ℓ.*26 genre「（芸術の）ジャンル」発音 〔ʒɑ́(:)nre | ʒɔ́n‐〕に注意／*ℓℓ.*29–30 Louise Beavers 米国で1920年代から1960年まで数多 くの映画やテレビに出演した俳優（1900-62）。／*ℓ.*32 draw on「動員する、利用する」／*ℓ.*36 the Nicholas Brothers フェイアードとハロルド兄弟によるダンスデュオ。／*ℓ.*38 Paul Robeson 多言 語で活躍した米国の俳優（1898-1976）。中国の国歌義勇軍行進曲を英訳したことでも有名。／*ℓ.*40 Harry Belafonte 米国の歌手、俳優（1927-2023）。アフリカ支援のチャリティソング "We are the World" の制作にも携わった。／*ℓ.*41 Sidney Poitier 黒人俳優の先駆者の一人。2022年に94歳で 死去。／*ℓ.*42 *Lilies of the Field* 邦題は『野のユリ』。放浪していた黒人青年が修道女たちと出会い、 教会堂を建設するまでの紆余曲折を描いた映画。／*ℓ.*43 recount「〜を詳しく述べる」

4 ▸ Vocabulary Check – 2nd Round ·····················

Choose the appropriate words below to fill in the blanks in the English sentences. Change forms if necessary.

| audience | exhibition | explore | primarily | star |

1. The advertisement is aimed _____ at children.

2. He _____ in a number of Hollywood action movies since he became an actor.

3. The director believes the series will attract a large female _____.

4. As prices have recently jumped, we need to _____ the possibility of cutting costs.

5. The paintings were sent to Hong Kong for _____.

5 ▸ True or False ·································

Read the following statements and indicate whether they are true (T) or not (F) along with the reasons. If you cannot determine T or F from the text, indicate NG (not given).

1. In the past, there used to be discrimination against black entertainers and filmmakers in Hollywood. **(T / F / NG)**

_____

2. African American audiences supported black filmmakers facing discrimination so that they could continue their jobs. **(T / F / NG)**

_____

3. Hollywood movies had started using more African American actors by the 1960s. **(T / F / NG)**

_____

6 ▶ Comprehension Check ··

Choose the best answer for each question.

1. What can visitors see in the exhibition?

    a. scripts, costumes, posters, and short films

    b. posters, short musicals, and cowboy films

    c. CDs, feature films, and juke boxes

2. Who was Louise Beavers?

    a. a filmmaker who made more than 100 films

    b. a performer who became very popular on the musical stage

    c. one of the actors who proved the talent of African American people

3. Which is true about Sidney Poitier?

    a. He made films featuring racial issues.

    b. He became a popular musical actor.

    c. He won an Oscar for best actor.

7 ▶ Retelling the Story ··

Re-tell the story presented in the video clip, including the following five keywords.

| a film museum | an exhibition | discrimination | black artists |

| many different genres |

_____

_____

8 ▶ Your Opinion in Writing ·····························

If you were a curator of the museum, what kind of exhibition would you like to plan? Why? Write at least six sentences.

_____

_____

_____

_____

_____

_____

9 **Further Information** ·································· 🔊 Audio 13

Read the passage below.

Asian Win in "Best Actress" Category a First

Michelle Yeoh's[*1] win in the Best Actress category marked a first for Asian representation at the Academy Awards, held Sunday night in Hollywood, Los Angeles. She was the first person of Asian descent to prevail[*2] in the category.

5 Looking only at the so-called Big Five categories, which are those considered the most prestigious, Oscar winners of Asian or Pacific Islander[*3] descent are more numerous than those from other racial or ethnic backgrounds. Especially in the last couple of years, Asian wins were recorded

10 in the categories Best Director, Best Picture or Best Screenplay[*4]. These included six wins total by Nomadland's

15 and Parasite's directors and producers Chloé Zhao[*5] and Bong Joon-ho[*6] as well as Jojo Rabbit's[*7] writer, Taika

20 Waititi[*8].

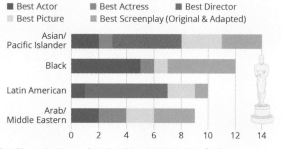

Asian Win in "Best Actress" Category a First

Wins in the Oscars' Big Five categories by individuals of the following races/ethnic backgrounds

■ Best Actor ■ Best Actress ■ Best Director
Best Picture ■ Best Screenplay (Original & Adapted)

Best Picture, Best Screenplay & Best Director: Participation of at least one person with aforementioned races/ethnic backgrounds
Sources: Academy of Motion Picture Arts and Sciences, Statista research

 statista ◪

© Statista

 Notes

[*1] **Michelle Yeoh** ハリウッドで活躍する中国系マレーシア人の女優（1962–）。／ [*2] **prevail** 「勝つ」
／ [*3] **Pacific Islander** 「太平洋諸島の人々」ミクロネシア、メラネシア、ポリネシアの人々を指す。／
[*4] **screenplay** 「脚本」／ [*5] **Chloé Zhao** 中国の映画監督、脚本家、映画プロデューサー（1982–）。
／ [*6] **Bong Joon-ho** 韓国の映画監督、脚本家（1969–）。／ [*7] **Jojo Rabbit** 米国のコメディ映画
（2019）。同作のサウンドトラックはグラミー賞を受賞。／ [*8] **Taika Waititi** ニュージーランドの映画監
督、テレビディレクター、脚本家、俳優、コメディアン（1975–）。

Vocabulary Checklist

Check the boxes after reviewing the meanings
of the words listed below.

Unit 6
Exhibition Explores Vibrant History of Black Filmmaking

☐ explore

☐ exhibition

☐ comprehensive

☐ primarily

☐ audience

☐ star

☐ feature film

☐ robust

☐ showcase

☐ imposing

New Research Suggests It's Time for a Digital Detox

みなさんはご自身が一日にどれくらいの時間、スマートフォンを見たり、インターネットに接続しているか計算してみたことはありますか？　ある企業が提供する「デジタル・デトックス・キャンプ」ではいったいどんなことをするのでしょうか。

 ## 1 Video Watching for Gist ·······················

Watch the video and pick up five keywords. Guess what the main theme (topic/issue) of the video clip is.

2 Vocabulary Check – 1st Round ····················

Match the following words and phrases with correct Japanese meanings.

1. impulse	・静寂
2. deliberately	・通知
3. serenity	・衝動
4. notification	・存在している
5. present	・意図的に

3 Video Watching & Script Reading 📶 Audio 14

Watch the video and fill in the appropriate words in the blanks.

Tom Cheshire: Spend a little time unconnected on the train or tube and more and more our first impulse is to reach for the phone. We are now online for more than one day each week. It's become so much that 34 percent of Internet users, 15 million of us, have tried a 'digital detox', deliberately logging off from connected devices.

Woman: Today, 1._____ 2._____ 3._____ people have said that they are hooked on these powerful portable devices, and I think it's that shift, that people are beginning to reflect on this, and deciding to get a bit of a breather.

Tom Cheshire: Every day we spend 8 hours and 45 minutes using media and communications—more time than we spend asleep.

Tom Cheshire: It's easy to feel digitally bombarded, especially now we are spending 25 hours a week online. In the 4._____ 5._____ alone I've had 27 work emails, 17 WhatsApp messages and eight text messages, thanks mom. And there's YouTube, Instagram, Facebook, Facebook Messenger, WeChat, Line, Kik, Twitter, Snapchat, Tinder, Bumble, Pinterest, and Pokémon Go.

It's no wonder we're looking for a bit of serenity.

Tom Cheshire: Whatever digital device you have, if you've got a TV

25 in your back pocket, I want **6.**＿＿＿＿＿＿ **7.**＿＿＿＿＿＿

well.

Tom Cheshire: In fact, companies have sprung up offering digital detox retreats where smartphones are banned and people have to do weird things like actually talk to each other. Or you could take another approach. To deal

30 with the problem of more technology, this East London company has invented another piece of technology. Their smart jewelry connects to your phone and filters its notifications, vibrating only for the most important contacts.

35 **Company representative:** We think technology makes you more productive, it does **8.**＿＿＿＿＿＿ **9.**＿＿＿＿＿＿

10.＿＿＿＿＿＿ good in the world but there's definitely finding the balance between using technology up to which point it's no longer productive anymore. It's

40 stressful, it's taking you out of being present, and being happy and being human, really.

Tom Cheshire: We're not all quite so abstemious, though. According to the report, just as many 15 million of us would definitely never like to do a detox. Tom Cheshire, Sky News.

📖✏️ **Notes**

Title **Digital Detox** 「デジタル・デトックス」detox は「解毒」の意。／ *ℓ.*1 **tube** ロンドンの地下鉄の愛称。筒状（tube）のトンネルからついた。正式名称は "The London Underground"。米国では地下鉄は subway と言うことが多い。／ *ℓ.*11 **breather** 「息抜き」／ *ℓ.*15 **digitally bombarded** 「デジタル攻めに遭う」／ *ℓℓ.*18–21 **WhatsApp, YouTube ... Pokémon Go** SNS等のアプリの名前。（2022年10月、アメリカの実業家イーロン・マスク氏が Twitter を買収し、2023年7月、ブランド名を「X」に変更した）／ *ℓ.*23 **TV** ここでは「液晶モニター付きのデバイス」のことを指している。／ *ℓℓ.*26–27 **digital detox retreat** 「デジタル・デトックス・キャンプ」retreat は「静修（期間）」の意味。／ *ℓ.*28 **weird** 《口語》「変な」／ *ℓ.*42 **abstemious** 「禁欲的な」

4 ▶ Vocabulary Check – 2nd Round ·······················

Choose the appropriate words below to fill in the blanks in the English sentences. Change forms if necessary.

ban	definitely	hooked on	reflect on	spring up

1. I need to _____ the situation before I make a final decision.

2. The movie was _____ in several countries due to inappropriate expressions.

3. Tim got _____ the show after watching the first episode.

4. Dozens of websites have _____ to provide information for travellers.

5. We are _____ against the idea of turning a park into a high-rise apartment building.

5 ▶ True or False ·······························

Read the following statements and indicate whether they are true (T) or not (F) along with the reasons. If you cannot determine T or F from the text, indicate NG (not given).

1. More than one-third of internet users have attempted to be unconnected from digital devices. **(T / F / NG)**

_____

2. We spend less time on sleep than on using digital devices. **(T / F / NG)**

_____

3. Companies have long offered digital detox retreats for people who use smartphones a lot. **(T / F / NG)**

_____

Comprehension Check ······························

Choose the best answer for each question.

1. What do the participants do at the digital detox retreat?

   a. They take classes on digital stress management.

   b. They learn how to control the use of digital devices.

   c. They hold conversations with other participants.

2. What is the purpose of smart jewellery?

   a. To keep record of the time people spend on their devices

   b. To prevent people from being disturbed by unimportant messages

   c. To notify people if they are using digital devices longer than they should

3. What is one negative impact of technology mentioned by an East London company representative?

   a. We focus so much on technology that we forget to live in the moment.

   b. We rely so much on technology that our jobs are being replaced by technology.

   c. We spend so much time with technology that our eyesight is getting worse.

 # Retelling the Story ·····························

Re-tell the story presented in the video clip, including the following five keywords.

`connected`　　`digital devices`　　`log off from`　　`a digital detox retreat`

`smart jewellery`

_____

_____

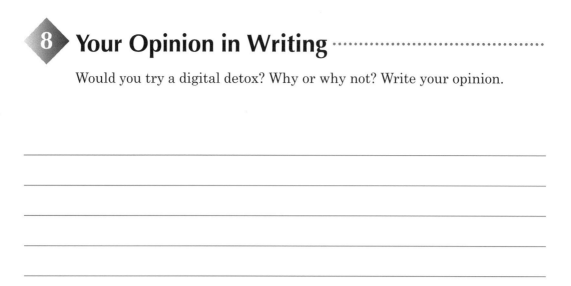

8 ▶ Your Opinion in Writing ·····························

Would you try a digital detox? Why or why not? Write your opinion.

_____

_____

_____

_____

_____

_____

9 Further Information ·· 🔊 Audio 15

Read the poster below.

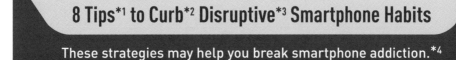

8 Tips*¹ to Curb*² Disruptive*³ Smartphone Habits

These strategies may help you break smartphone addiction.*⁴

Prioritize*⁵ self-care
through mindfulness*⁶

Exercise, like going
for a run or walk

Schedule no-screen
time daily

Turn off social media
notifications

Take a digital detox

Spend time with
family

Use apps that limit
screen time

Learn new things, or
take on*⁷ a hobby

Notes

*¹ **tip**「ヒント」／ *² **curb**「～を抑制する」／ *³ **disruptive**「破壊的な」／ *⁴ **addiction**「中毒」／ *⁵ **prioritize**「～を優先する」／ *⁶ **mindfulness**「マインドフルネス」今起きていることに注意を向ける瞑想法。／ *⁷ **take on**「～を始める」

Vocabulary Checklist

Check the boxes after reviewing the meanings
of the words listed below.

Unit 7
New Research Suggests It's Time for a Digital Detox

- ☐ impulse
- ☐ deliberately
- ☐ hook on
- ☐ reflect on
- ☐ serenity

- ☐ spring up
- ☐ ban
- ☐ notification
- ☐ definitely
- ☐ present (adj.)

Afghan Girls Cling to Dreams as Taliban Continue Education Ban

▶▶▶

2021年8月にアフガニスタンで政権を握った武装勢力タリバンの高等教育省が、大学での女性への教育を停止するという通知をしました。ファイサルさんは自国の人々が医療を求めて国外へ出ずに済むよう医師になる夢を持っていましたが、彼女のその夢は今、単なる夢になってしまっているというのです。

1 Video Watching for Gist

Watch the video and pick up five keywords. Guess what the main theme (topic/issue) of the video clip is.

2 Vocabulary Check – 1st Round

Match the following words and phrases with correct Japanese meanings.

1. management	・	部門
2. sector	・	（好機を）待つ
3. acceptable	・	この件について
4. in this regard	・	受け入れられる
5. bide	・	経営

3 Video Watching & Script Reading 🔊 Audio 16

Watch the video and fill in the appropriate words in the blanks.

Reporter: One year ago, 19-year-old Shiba Faisal had no idea that she would be forced to stay at home and no longer attend school. The Taliban, which rose 1._____ 2._____ in August of 2021, placed a ban on girls' education. Faisal was in the 12th grade.

5

Shiba Faisal: I wanted to become a doctor so that people of my country wouldn't be forced to go abroad for treatment. But unfortunately, that dream 3._____ 4._____ remains just a dream that is headed for destruction because now we can't go to school.

10

Reporter: Her older sister, Nilofar Faisal worked in the management sector for a private company. Now she is also being 5._____ 6._____ stay at home.

Nilofar Faisal: Life without a job is very painful, especially when you are supporting yourself as a student and your family. I'm in very bad condition, like a walking-dead person.

15

Reporter: The Taliban has ordered women like the Faisal sisters 7._____ 8._____ many institutions to stay at home. The Taliban say they support girls' education and that they will soon clarify their position on the matter and reopen the girls' schools.

20

Zabihullah Mujahid: The issue of girls' education is being worked on. We want a solution that is acceptable 9._____ 10._____ . We are making efforts in this regard and it will be done soon.

25

Reporter: However, Shiba Faisal is not ready to believe the Taliban's claims.

Shiba Faisal: I think these people will always make some excuse and deceive us. I don't think our schools will open.

30 **Reporter:** Despite not attending school, Shiba Faisal keeps herself busy. She has turned to poetry and says many of her friends have started to stay active by doing things like carpet weaving, sewing, embroidery and handicrafts, biding time and hoping one day they will be able to
35 resume their studies and pursue their dreams. For Nazar Ul Islam in Kabul, Afghanistan, Bezhan Hamdard, VOA News.

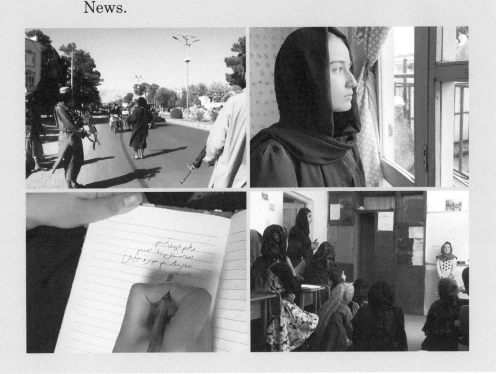

Notes

Title **cling to**「～にしがみつく、こだわる」／ *ℓℓ.*6–7 **so that ... not ~**「…が～しないように」／ *ℓ.*9 **destruction**「破滅」／ *ℓ.*16 **walking-dead**「生ける屍（しかばね）」／ *ℓ.*18 **institution**「（公共）施設」／ *ℓ.*28 **make some excuse**「何らかの言い訳をする」／ *ℓ.*29 **deceive**「欺く、裏切る」／ *ℓ.*33 **weave**「織る、作る」／ *ℓ.*33 **embroidery**「刺繍」

Vocabulary Check – 2nd Round

Choose the appropriate words below to fill in the blanks in the English sentences. Change forms if necessary.

| clarify | claim | deceive | resume | pursue |

1. He tried to _____ his friends by pretending to be someone else.

2. This political _____ is not believed anymore.

3. I am pleased to _____ my position.

4. After taking a break, she plans to _____ her studies and complete her degree.

5. She decided to _____ her dream as a singer.

5 **True or False**

Read the following statements and indicate whether they are true (T) or not (F) along with the reason. If you cannot determine T or F from the text, indicate NG (not given).

1. The Taliban has prohibited girls' education in Afghanistan.   (T / F / NG)

_____

2. The Taliban is not going to support girls' education.   (T / F / NG)

_____

3. Shiba Faisal does not believe the Taliban's claims about equal job opportunities for women.   (T / F / NG)

_____

Comprehension Check ··

Choose the best answer for each question.

1. Why was Shiba Faisal's dream to be a doctor?

    a. because she wanted to be famous in her community

    b. because she did not want people to be forced to go abroad for treatment

    c. because she was raised by parents who are doctors

2. Why is life without a job particularly challenging for Nilofer Faisal?

    a. because she has to support herself and her family

    b. because she has no interest in pursuing a career

    c. because she lacks the necessary qualifications for employment

3. How do Shiba Faisal and her friends spend their time without school?

    a. By participating in sports events held in the city

    b. By doing some activities like poetry and handicrafts

    c. By volunteering in their community as a teacher

 Retelling the Story ································

Re-tell the story presented in the video clip, including the following five keywords.

| Taliban | ban girls' education | attend school | was forced to |

| reopen schools |

_____

_____

8 ▶ Your Opinion in Writing ······························

Do you think there is equal career opportunity or educational equality between men and women in Japan?

_____

_____

_____

_____

_____

_____

9 ▶ Further Information ······················ 🔊 Audio 17

Read the passage and the checklist below.

How does UNESCO*¹ support education in Afghanistan?

UNESCO has been strongly involved in supporting the education system in Afghanistan during the last 20 years, including running a successful literacy*² programme that reached over 600,000 youth and adults. 60% of the beneficiaries*³ were women.

5   Since August 2021, UNESCO has shifted its interventions*⁴ to ensure continuity of education through community-based*⁵ literacy and skills development classes for over 25,000 youth and adults, including 60% women and adolescent*⁶ girls in 20 provinces*⁷. Its advocacy*⁸ campaign "Literacy for a Brighter Future" reached out

10   to over 20 million Afghans to increase public awareness of the right to education for youth and adults, especially women and adolescent girls.

Afghan girls at school in Herat. Afghanistan 2019.
© solmaz daryani/ Shutterstock.com

　　UNESCO is also working on an education data monitoring initiative to ensure reliable data so that education partners
15　channel*9 funding to the most critical and unmet education needs.

📖 Notes

*1 **UNESCO** ユネスコは 1946 年に設立され、異なる文明、文化、国民の間の対話をもたらすための活動をしている。／ *2 **literacy**「読み書きの能力、識字能力」上の写真は読み書きを学んでいる様子。／ *3 **beneficiary**「恩恵を受ける人」／ *4 **intervention**「介入」／ *5 **community-based**「地域密着型の」／ *6 **adolescent**「（子供から大人に成長している）思春期の」／ *7 **province**「州」／ *8 **advocacy**「支援運動」／ *9 **channel**「投入する」

Vocabulary Checklist

Check the boxes after reviewing the meanings of the words listed below.

Unit 8
Afghan Girls Cling to Dreams
as Taliban Continue Education Ban

☐ management

☐ sector

☐ clarify

☐ acceptable

☐ in this regard

☐ claim

☐ deceive

☐ bide

☐ resume

☐ pursue

Equal Pay Day Reminder of Pay Disparity Between Men, Women

▶▶▶

日本では、男性一般労働者の給与水準を100とした場合、女性一般労働者の給与水準は75.2%です。日本は諸外国と比較しても、男女の賃金格差の割合は大きい状況にあります。アメリカの状況はどうなのでしょうか。米国政府のこれまでの、そして今後の対策と合わせて見ていきましょう。

1 Video Watching for Gist

Watch the video and pick up five keywords. Guess what the main theme (topic/issue) of the video clip is.

2 Vocabulary Check – 1st Round

Match the following words and phrases with correct Japanese meanings.

1. commemorate	・（法、制度などを）復活させる
2. hamper	・公平
3. equity	・〜を記念する
4. administration	・〜を阻止する
5. reinstate	・政権

Watch the video and fill in the appropriate words in the blanks.

Reporter: In many sectors, including food industry and science, American women earn less than men. On average, an American woman makes only $0.83 for every dollar earned by a man. The gap is even greater for black
5   women, native American women, Latinas and certain subpopulations of Asian women.

Reporter: On March 15, President Joe Biden commemorated the day that symbolizes how long women must work to earn what men earned the previous year. In 2021, Equal Pay
10   Day fell on March 24th. The pandemic has hampered progress, with women doing most of the family caregiving as they deal with children learning virtually, and older family members losing access to care.

Joe Biden: I signed an executive order to promote **1.**_____
15   **2.**_____ **3.**_____ pay equality, pay equity for employees of federal contractors, and it's my hope that this **4.**_____ **5.**_____ **6.**_____ for all private companies to follow as well.

Reporter: The actions Biden announced do not address the
20   gender wage gap in the private sector. The Obama administration required large companies to report how much they pay workers by race and gender, but the Trump administration, under pressure from big

business groups, halted the rule in 2017.

25 **Vasu Reddy:** The Biden administration is analyzing the data 7.＿＿＿＿＿＿ 8.＿＿＿＿＿＿ collected from private companies to show the wage gaps by race and gender. This is hopefully the first step in 9.＿＿＿＿＿ 10.＿＿＿＿＿ rule reinstated.

30 **Reporter:** Also Tuesday, Kamala Harris, the first female American vice president, hosted an Equal Pay Day virtual summit attended by administration officials, athletes, and CEOs.

Kamala Harris: An economy that works for women and for everyone.

35 **Reporter:** Some argue that mandating paid leave for new parents could help narrow the gender pay gap. The U.S. is the only developed nation in the world without a national paid parental leave program.

Adrienne Schweer: One in four women in America are said to go back 40 to work within 10 to 14 days of giving birth, which is astonishing and awful. It is terrible for working women.

Reporter: Biden's proposed Build Back Better Act seeks to provide national paid family leave. But the massive $2 trillion social spending bill is struggling to gain approval in 45 Congress. Patsy Widakuswara, VOA News, Washington.

📖✏️ **Notes**

Title **Equal Pay Day**「平等賃金の日」1月1日に男女が同時に働き始めた場合、1年間で女性が男性と同じ賃金を得るためには、年を越して多く働かねばならなならないと言われており、賃金が同額に達する日を指す。／*ℓ*.5 **Latina**「（米国に住む）ラテン系アメリカ人女性」男性はLatino。／*ℓ*.6 **subpopulation**「集団の一部」／*ℓ*.13 **access to care** 直訳では「介護へのアクセス」となるが、ここでは「デイケアセンターなどでの介護サービス」の意味となる。／*ℓ*.14 **executive order**「行政命令」／*ℓ*.16 **federal contractor**「連邦の契約団体」米国では、federalは合衆国全体を指す。／*ℓ*.20 **private sector**「民間企業」sectorは「（事業・産業の）部門、分野」の意。／*ℓ*.42 **Build Back Better Act**「ビルド・バック・ベター（より良い復興）法案」米国での中産階級を再建し、生活と労働環境を改善するために、バイデン政権によって提案された法案。／*ℓ*.45 **congress**「米国議会」上院（the Senate）と下院（the House of Representatives）から成る。英国議会はParliament、日本の国会は the Diet。

4 ▶ Vocabulary Check – 2nd Round ·····················

Choose the appropriate words below to fill in the blanks in the English sentences. Change forms if necessary.

| wage | halt | mandate | leave | approval |

1. Many people work multiple jobs to increase their _____ .

2. The driver _____ the car at the red traffic light.

3. She eagerly awaited her parents' _____ of her career choice.

4. The law _____ weekly physical education hours for all students.

5. She is taking a two-week _____ to care for her newborn baby.

5 ▶ True or False ··

Read the following statements and indicate whether they are true (T) or not (F) along with the reasons. If you cannot determine T or F from the text, indicate NG (not given).

1. Big differences in payment exist between black women, native American women and Latinas.   **(T / F / NG)**

_____

2. As women needed to spend their time taking care of their family members during the pandemic, they could not earn the same amount of money as men did.   **(T / F / NG)**

_____

3. Setting national paid parental leave aims to encourage more parents to take leave.   **(T / F / NG)**

_____

66

Comprehension Check ···

Choose the best answer for each question.

1. Which administration stopped reporting wage differences by race and gender under pressure from big business?

   a. the Biden administration

   b. the Obama administration

   c. the Trump administration

2. What is surprising and terrible about 25% of women in the US?

   a. returning to the same job that they used to have before they were pregnant

   b. not being able to rest enough after giving birth

   c. taking care of their families in addition to new-born babies

3. Why is the proposed national paid family leave difficult to get approved?

   a. because it will not contribute to gender pay equality

   b. because the content of the proposal is not good enough

   c. because it costs a huge amount of money to carry out

 Retelling the Story ···

Re-tell the story presented in the video clip, including the following five keywords.

   gender and racial   wage gaps   the Biden administration   propose

   a national paid family leave

_____

_____

8 ▶ Your Opinion in Writing ·····························

If you were to live with someone in the future, what part of housework would you be in charge of? Write at least six sentences.

9 ◆ **Further Information** .... 🔊 **Audio 19**

Read the passage below.

Equal Pay for Work of Equal Value

Worldwide, women only make 77 cents for every dollar earned by men. As a result, there's a lifetime of income inequality between men and women and more women are retiring into poverty.

This stubborn[*1] inequality in the average wages between men 5 and women persists in all countries and across all sectors, because women's work is under-valued and women tend to be concentrated in different jobs than men. Even though the work itself may require equal or more effort and skills, it's valued and remunerated[*2] less. For women of colour[*3], immigrant women and mothers, the gap 10 widens. The so-called "motherhood penalty[*4]" pushes women into informal economy[*5], casual[*6] and part-time work, and tends to be larger in developing countries than in developed countries.

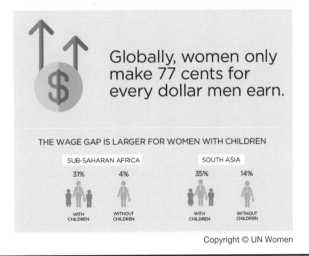

Copyright © UN Women

 Notes

*1 stubborn「変わることのない」／***2 remunerate**「報酬を与える」／***3 colour** ここでは「色」ではなく肌の色を指して「有色人種の」の意。《米》color ／***4 motherhood penalty**「母親ペナルティ」「働く母親は子供のいない女性と比較して、賃金、認識される能力、福利厚生の面で不利である」という現象を指す。／***5 informal economy**「インフォーマル経済」公式な取り決めの適用を十分に受けていない労働者によるすべての経済活動を指す。個人事業主や家事労働、路上販売などが含まれる。／***6 casual**「（仕事が）臨時雇いの」

Vocabulary Checklist

Check the boxes after reviewing the meanings
of the words listed below.

Unit 9
Equal Pay Day Reminder of Pay Disparity Between Men, Women

☐ commemorate   ☐ administration

☐ hamper   ☐ reinstate

☐ equity   ☐ mandate

☐ wage   ☐ leave (n.)

☐ halt   ☐ approval

New York School Offers Dual-Language Instruction

▶▶▶

ニューヨークという都市は文化的にも社会的にも多様化しています。ニューヨーク市教育局は、16万人の英語学習者を2カ国語で指導するプログラムを実施しています。2歳でアメリカにやって来たロシア人のフディコヴァさんの両親はとても喜んでいるといいます。なぜなのでしょうか。

 ## Video Watching for Gist

Watch the video and pick up five keywords. Guess what the main theme (topic/issue) of the video clip is.

 ## Vocabulary Check – 1st Round

Match the following words and phrases with correct Japanese meanings.

1. diverse	・統合する
2. integrate	・経済的な
3. economical	・多様性のある
4. middle school	・必ずしも〜ない
5. not necessarily	・中学校

3 Video Watching & Script Reading 🔊 Audio 20

Watch the video and fill in the appropriate words in the blanks.

Reporter: It's no easy task to serve more than 1 million students who speak almost 200 languages while providing equal services for all. But New York's Department of Education makes school a **1.**_____ **2.**_____

5 for its 160,000 English language learners through its dual language programs.

Milady Baez: We have to understand that our city has become extremely diverse, and that we also need to prepare our students for jobs **3.**_____ **4.**_____

10 **5.**_____. The jobs of the future require that our students know more than one language. They're going to be traveling abroad. They're going to be communicating with people from all over the world. This will open doors for them.

15 **Reporter:** Dual language programs integrate students culturally and linguistically. Math, social studies, science, and all other regular courses are taught in both languages. David A. Boody Middle School in Brooklyn offers dual language instruction in Russian, Mandarin, Spanish and

20 Hebrew. Teacher Shuya Zhang says the dual language program prepares children for a globalized world.

Shuya Zhang: So they have both the languages, they can get more opportunities. Look at nowadays. America started economical relationships with China. Lots of

25 factories had been built, car companies **6.**_____ **7.**_____ China. They need people with the skills. With both the language skills. So, the kids, when they grow up, they already have this skill.

Reporter: But middle school students are not necessarily worried

30   about finding jobs. For Kequing Jaing, it's just a comfort
          to maintain her first language, Mandarin.

Kequing Jaing: It makes me like, feel that I'm home because I
          can speak in Chinese learn in Chinese while learning
          in English. So it makes me feel better and makes

35   me understand more **8.**_____ **9.**_____
          10._____ I'm learning.

Reporter: Russian English student Anastasia Hudikova arrived
          in the United States at the age of two. She says the
          program helps maintain her heritage and keeps her

40   parents happy.

Anastasia Hudikova: They're really happy about the program that
          it exists. They're really happy that I can preserve my
          culture and my language, that I can speak it fluently in
          school.

45 **Reporter:** Systemwide, New York Schools offer instruction in
          eight other languages: Arabic, Bengali, French, Haitian
          Creole, Yiddish, Korean, Hebrew and Polish, with plans
          to add even more in the future. Michael Lehmann, VOA
          News, New York.

Notes

***Title* dual**「2つの」／**ℓℓ.3–4 New York's Department of Education**「ニューヨーク州教育局」米国では州により教育制度が異なる。／**ℓ.16 linguistically**「言語的に」／**ℓ.16 social studies**「（教科としての）社会科」／**ℓ.18 Brooklyn** ニューヨーク州の区の1つ。／**ℓ.19 Mandarin**「標準中国語」／**ℓ.20 Hebrew**「ヘブライ語」イスラエルで話されている。／**ℓ.33 speak in Chinese learn in Chinese** 1つ目のChineseの後にandが省略されている。／**ℓ.39 heritage**「（受け継がれる文化・歴史的）伝統」／**ℓ.46 Arabic**「アラビア語」／**ℓ.46 Bengali**「ベンガル語」主にバングラディシュで話されている。／**ℓℓ.46–47 Haitian Creole**「ハイチ・クレオール語あるいはハイチ語」クレオールとは2言語の接触から生まれたPidgin（ピジン語）が母語化したもの。／**ℓ.47 Yiddish**「イディッシュ語」米国や東欧などのユダヤ人移民の間で話される。ヘブライ文字で書かれる。／**ℓ.47 Polish**「ポーランド語」

Vocabulary Check – 2nd Round ·····················

Choose the appropriate words below to fill in the blanks in the English sentences. Change forms if necessary.

| equal | extremely | instruction | preserve | fluently |

1. Rights and opportunities should be _____ for all individuals, regardless of their background.

2. It is important to _____ our natural resources for future generations.

3. He speaks English _____ after living in an English-speaking country for several years.

4. This school provides personalized _____ for each student.

5. The weather was _____ hot, making it difficult to stay outside for long.

True or False ··

Read the following statements and indicate whether they are true (T) or not (F) along with the reasons. If you cannot determine T or F from the text, indicate NG (not given).

1. New York's Department of Education serves more than one million students who speak almost 200 languages. **(T / F / NG)**

_____

2. Dual language programs require a lot of money to hire more native speakers as language teachers. **(T / F / NG)**

_____

3. Anastasia Hudikova does not believe that the dual language program helps to keep her parents happy. **(T / F / NG)**

_____

Comprehension Check ···

Choose the best answer for each question.

1. How are regular courses, such as math, social studies, and science, taught in dual language programs?

   a. only in English to promote students' fluency and future social status

   b. only in the students' native language to maintain cultural heritage

   c. in both languages to integrate students culturally and linguistically

2. Why does Kequing Jaing find comfort in the dual language program?

   a. because it helps her find future employment opportunities

   b. because it allows her to use her mother tongue

   c. because it offers financial incentives and scholarships

3. How many languages are currently offered for instruction in New York Schools?

   a. 4 languages

   b. 12 languages

   c. 15 languages

 Retelling the Story ···································

Re-tell the story presented in the video clip, including the following five keywords.

dual language programs ·   a globalized world   job opportunities

comfort   feel more at home

8 ▶ Your Opinion in Writing ·····················

How can teaching classes in English and Japanese benefit English learners living in Japan in their future education and career?

_____

_____

_____

_____

_____

_____

9 ▶ Further Information ····················· Audio 21

Read the passage below.

Japan Public Elementary School Offers Rare English-Immersion Program

---

At Haccho elementary school in Toyohashi, Aichi Prefecture, English is the dominant language for a special class in each grade. It is used throughout the curriculum except for Japanese language and ethics[1] classes, and Japanese is only used when a teacher has
5　to explain the meaning of a word.

The city of Toyohashi, which is home to a number of[2] foreign residents[3] and is a member of the council of municipalities[4] with a large number of foreign residents, has put a lot of effort into[5] English education.

10　'There are challenges in supporting teachers and providing financial assistance, but there is a significance in realizing such

classes at public elementary schools in which pupils with diverse backgrounds attend,' said Tetsuo Harada, a Waseda University professor and an advisor at the World Family's Institute of
15 Bilingual Science[*6], which supports the school.

Harada added six years of elementary school education is not enough for students to learn all subjects in English, saying, "We need to work with junior and senior high schools."

「ひと・まち・東海」公立小で異例　〝英語漬け〟主に英語で実施された算数の授業＝2022年6月13日、愛知県豊橋市の市立八町小　Photo：Kyodo News

 Notes

[*1] **ethics** 「道徳」／[*2] **a number of** 「多くの」／[*3] **resident** 「居住者」／[*4] **council of municipalities** 「自治体国際化協会」／[*5] **put effort into** 「〜に取り組む」／[*6] **World Family's Institute of Bilingual Science** 「ワールド・ファミリー バイリンガル サイエンス研究所」日本でのバイリンガル教育（英語と日本語）の研究機関。

Vocabulary Checklist

Check the boxes after reviewing the meanings
of the words listed below.

Unit 10
New York School Offers Dual-Language Instruction

☐ equal   ☐ instruction

☐ extremely   ☐ economical

☐ diverse   ☐ not necessarily

☐ integrate   ☐ preserve

☐ middle school   ☐ fluently

Could Gene Edited Plants Play a Key Part in Helping to Improve Global Food Inequality?

▶▶▶

CRISPR-Cas9という遺伝子編集技術があります。動画に登場するトマトは普通のトマトに見えますが、実はこの技術によってトマトのDNAに手を加え、豊富なビタミンDを含んでいるのです。この技術は従来の遺伝子組み換えとは根本的に異なります。その違いはどんなものなのでしょうか。そして、この技術の重要性とは？

1 Video Watching for Gist

Watch the video and pick up five keywords. Guess what the main theme (topic/issue) of the video clip is.

2 Vocabulary Check – 1st Round

Match the following words and phrases with correct Japanese meanings.

1. genetically	・〜を与える
2. equivalent	・途方もなく
3. tweak	・同等のこと
4. prohibitively	・微調整する、操作する
5. confer	・遺伝子学的に

Video Watching & Script Reading Audio 22

Watch the video and fill in the appropriate words in the blanks.

Reporter: They don't look any different to ordinary tomatoes, which is very much the point. But these have been genetically 1._____ 2._____ 3._____ high levels of vitamin D. Normal tomatoes like most fruits and veg contain
5   virtually none. But just 4._____ 5._____ these has as much vitamin D as two eggs, or a serving of tuna. They used a gene editing technique called CRISPR-Cas9 to tweak the tomatoes' DNA.

Cathie Martin: We talk about genetic tweezes, so it really is very
10   very small. Nature equivalents, they can happen naturally or could happen naturally, but the amount of work and time required to make that change and then select it and breed it is prohibitively long.

Reporter: The technique is fundamentally different to previous
15   incarnations of genetic modification, or GM. Most GM products contain genes from another organism that confer a benefit. A type of GM cotton, for example, has a gene from a bacterium to make it resistant to insect pests. By contrast, gene editing inserts molecular machinery borrowed from bacteria to delete,
20   swap, or repeat genes already in the plant's genetic code before removing the foreign DNA afterwards.

Reporter: The difference is a crucial one, because this week, the government will put forward a bill making it much easier to bring gene-edited crops to market. And they're closer than you
25   might think.

Tom Clarke: This plot is the first crop of gene-edited wheat grown anywhere outdoors in Europe. And the researchers behind it hope this change in the law will be the first step to taking crops like this out of field trials and seeing them benefit society.

30 **Nigel Halford:** It's the first positive step in crop biotechnology

regulation in Europe, in the UK for a generation, 25 years. And I've suffered all through that period. We've been 6._____ 7._____ this for a long time, and I think it's really a positive step.

35 **Reporter:** This wheat has been edited to make less of the cancer-causing compound, acrylamide, when it's fried. The researchers are also looking at editing out common wheat allergens or making the crop more drought or pest resistant.

Nigel Halford: It's really 8._____ 9._____ 10._____

40 don't miss out on the next bio-tech revolution, which is gene editing. And that is already off and running in some parts of the world. United States, for example, several years, Canada, Brazil, Argentina... Just this year we see China and India moving on biotech, on gene editing, so really important that 45 we keep up.

Reporter: But opponents of gene editing dispute claimed similarities to traditional breeding and say the law change is a step towards more elaborate genetic engineering.

Pat Thomas: It's entirely misleading to say that gene editing 50 doesn't involve the insertion of foreign genes. In fact, gene editing is a suite of technologies that range from a simple snip to the complex insertion of foreign genes, and the traits that get scientists really excited, things like disease resistance and drought resistance, simply cannot be achieved without these 55 complex technological interventions.

Reporter: With gene editing, scientists have proven they've got a tool that can revolutionize food and farming, but they have some way to go to prove real benefits to society and the environment. Tom Clarke, Sky News, Norwich.

📖 Notes

l.1 **tomatoes** 英国風の発音 [təmάːtoʊz] に注意。／*l*.7 **CRISPR-Cas9** 「クリスパー・キャス9」遺伝子情報（ゲノム）を自在に変えられる技術。狙ったゲノムの場所を簡単に改変できる点が最大の特徴と言われる。／*l*.9 **genetic tweezes** 「遺伝子をピンセットでつまむようなこと」／*l*.15 **incarnation** 「具体化」／*l*.18 **insect pest** 「害虫」pest のみで同義となる場合もある。／*l*.19 **molecular machinery** 「分子機構」／*l*.36 **acrylamide** 「アクリルアミド」／*l*.37 **allergen** 「アレルゲン」アレルギーの原因となる物質を指す。／*l*.48 **elaborate** 「複雑な」／*l*.51 **a suite of** 「一連の」／*l*.51 **snip** 「断片、少量」／*l*.52 **trait** 「特徴」

4 ▶ Vocabulary Check – 2nd Round ·····················

Choose the appropriate words below to fill in the blanks in the English sentences. Change forms if necessary.

dispute   drought   opponent   ordinary   resistant

1. I prefer _____ days filled with simple pleasures.

2. This plant is _____ to cold and grows both outdoors and indoors.

3. The farmers struggled with little crop due to the long _____ .

4. Our _____ played tough, but we won in the end.

5. They had a _____ over who should be the group leader.

5 ▶ True or False ·····························

Read the following statements and indicate whether they are true (T) or not (F) along with the reasons. If you cannot determine T or F from the text, indicate NG (not given).

1. One advantage of gene editing is to produce foods with high quality by spending more time.   (T / F / NG)

_____

2. It took 25 years for the UK government to have a bill approved for allowing gene-edited products on market.   (T / F / NG)

_____

3. Some people are opposed to gene editing because it is similar to GM.   (T / F / NG)

_____

6 Comprehension Check ·····································

Choose the best answer for each question.

1. What is the difference between GM and gene-editing?

    a. the frequency of swapping genes

    b. the degree of resistance to insects

    c. permanent insertion of foreign DNA or not

2. What sort of wheat is expected to be invented?

    a. wheat without cancer-causing compound

    b. wheat causing no allergy

    c. wheat which isn't strong against drought

3. Why does Pat Thomas mention disease resistance and drought resistance?

    a. to explain that crops with these traits actually require GM, not gene editing

    b. to demonstrate that gene editing ranges from a simple snip to the complex insertion of foreign genes

    c. to insist that complex technological interventions require a large amount of time

7 Retelling the Story ·······································

Re-tell the story presented in the video clip, including the following five keywords.

| inserts | genes from another organism | remove | put forward a bill |

| market |

8 ▶ Your Opinion in Writing ·······················

What kind of gene-edited products would like to have in the future? Why?
Write at least six sentences.

9 ▶ **Further Information** ⋯⋯⋯⋯⋯⋯⋯⋯⋯⋯ Audio 23

Read the passage below.

Gene Edited Crops Must be Registered*¹, But Do Not Require Safety or Environmental Testing

Japan is a major importer and consumer of crops derived from*² biotechnology—it imports close to 100% of their corn and 94% of their soybean supply—but domestic production remains extremely limited. The advent*³ of gene editing appears to be
5　transforming the country's view of genetic modification.

Japan is emerging as a pioneer in the introduction of gene-edited foodstuffs*⁴. It allows gene-edited products to be sold to consumers without safety evaluations as long as the techniques involved meet certain criteria*⁵—a screening process similar
10　to that adopted by the United States. It has introduced three CRISPR*⁶-edited products to date: fleshier*⁷ red sea bream*⁸, high-growth tiger puffer*⁹, and a GABA-enriched tomato. Referred to in the media as a 'super tomato', it features*¹⁰ five times the normal amount of GABA, an amino acid*¹¹ linked
15　to lower blood pressure*¹², thanks to tweaks to genes that normally limit GABA production.

 Notes

*¹ **register**「～を登録する」／*² **derived from**「～由来の」／*³ **advent**「出現、到来」／*⁴ **foodstuff** 「食材、食品」／*⁵ **criteria**「基準」criterionの複数形。／*⁶ **CRISPR**「クリスパー」DNAの中の特定の集合体。／*⁷ **fleshier**「より肉厚な」fleshyの比較級。／*⁸ **red sea bream**「真鯛」／*⁹ **tiger puffer**「トラフグ」／*¹⁰ **feature**「～を含む」／*¹¹ **amino acid**「アミノ酸」／*¹² **lower blood pressure**「低血圧」

Vocabulary Checklist

Check the boxes after reviewing the meanings
of the words listed below.

Unit 11
Could Gene Edited Plants Play a Key Part in Helping to Improve Global Food Inequality?

☐ ordinary

☐ genetically

☐ tweak

☐ equivalent

☐ prohibitively

☐ confer

☐ resistant

☐ drought

☐ opponent

☐ dispute

Unit *12*

New Supersonic Plane

超音速飛行というものをご存知ですか？　1970年代に超音速機コンコルドが登場し、技術の驚異と言われながらも、2003年に商業運行を終えて20年が経過したのですが……。

1 Video Watching for Gist

Watch the video and pick up five keywords. Guess what the main theme (topic/issue) of the video clip is.

2 Vocabulary Check – 1st Round

Match the following words and phrases with correct Japanese meanings.

1. marvel	・航空
2. operational	・大気
3. sustainable	・運用の
4. aviation	・持続可能な
5. atmosphere	・驚異

3 Video Watching & Script Reading 🔊 Audio 24

Watch the video and fill in the appropriate words in the blanks.

Reporter: When the Concorde supersonic airplane first appeared on the scene in the 1970s, it was considered a technological marvel. The planes, a joint Anglo-French venture, traveled 1._____ 2._____ than twice the

5 speed of sound, cutting transatlantic flight times by half. When they were retired in 2003, mainly due to unsustainable operational costs and complaints about the thunderous sonic boom, nothing took their place. Until now.

10 **Reporter:** US based United Airlines has partnered with Boom Supersonic Aerospace Company of Denver, Colorado, to purchase 15 supersonic aircraft 3._____ 4._____ 5._____ for more. Boom's Overture Aircraft will also cut transatlantic flying time by 50% but

15 will be quieter than the Concorde and more sustainable, the firm says.

Blake Scholl (Company CEO): We have computer optimization techniques so we can design a far more efficient

20   aerodynamic shape versus having to iterate slowly through wind tunnels. And we've had complete re-architecture of how jet engines work. I want to get to the point where a supersonic ticket is actually cheaper than subsonic.

Man: The Concorde failed not because it wasn't technically
25   feasible. It failed 6._____ 7._____ the cost. But we think this is going to be 75% less costly than operating the Concorde.

Reporter: The Overture aircraft will run on 100% sustainable aviation fuel.

30 **Blake Scholl:** Which means that supersonic flights are going to be 100% carbon neutral. Effectively, we're taking carbon out of the atmosphere, convert it into jet fuel and then we burn it in the airplane. It just goes right back where it came from.

35 **Reporter:** While supersonic flight is a technological achievement, the company says it's really about saving people time.

Blake Scholl: Because ultimately it's about being on the ground on the planet with people who matter, not about 8._____ 9._____ 10._____ the sky.

40 **Reporter:** Boom is planning to build and deliver its planes to United by the end of the decade. Julie Taboh, VOA News.

📖✏️ **Notes**

Title **supersonic**「超音速の」／ℓ.1 **Concorde supersonic airplane**「コンコルド超音速旅客機」／ℓ.3 **Anglo-French**「英仏の」／ℓ.3 **venture**「合弁事業」／ℓ.5 **transatlantic**「大西洋横断の」／ℓ.8 **thunderous**「(雷のように) とどろきわたる」／ℓ.8 **sonic boom**「ソニック・ブーム」航空機が超音速で飛行する時に発生させる衝撃波によって起こる大音響。／ℓ.11 **Denver** コロラド州の州都。／ℓℓ.17–18 **computer optimization technique**「コンピュータ最適化技術」／ℓ.19 **aerodynamic shape**「空気力学的 (空気力学の原理を応用した) 形状」／ℓ.19 **versus ~**「~に対して」／ℓ.19 **iterate**「何度も繰り返す」／ℓ.20 **wind tunnel**「風洞」人工的に空気の流れを加減できるようにした実験装置。／ℓ.23 **subsonic**「音速以下の、亜音速 (機) の」ここでは通常の航空機を指す。／ℓ.31 **carbon neutral**「カーボンニュートラルな」人間が排出する二酸化炭素量を植物の二酸化炭素吸収量などと相殺し、ゼロになっている状態。／ℓ.31 **effectively**「実質的に」／ℓ.32 **convert ~ into ...**「~を…に変える」

4 ▶ Vocabulary Check – 2nd Round ··

Choose the appropriate words below to fill in the blanks in the English sentences. Change forms if necessary.

| complaint | convert | costly | retire | ultimately |

1. The last Shinkansen series Zero _____ in a special farewell ceremony at Hakata Station in 2008.

2. It's important to listen to your parents, but _____, you'll have to decide for yourself.

3. We are going to _____ our son's bedroom to a guest room.

4. It is _____ to make all university facilities barrier-free.

5. Working in the Customer Service Department, I have to deal with customer _____ every day.

5 ▶ True or False ··

Read the following statements and indicate whether they are true (T) or not (F) along with the reasons. If you cannot determine T or F from the text, indicate NG (not given).

1. No supersonic aircraft have flown for two years.　　　　　(T / F / NG)

_____

2. The cost of operating the Overture aircraft will be a quarter of that of the Concorde supersonic aircraft.　　　　　(T / F / NG)

_____

3. Lower price for the new supersonic plane will attract more passengers.
　　　　　(T / F / NG)

_____

6 Comprehension Check ·······························

Choose the best answer for each question.

1. Which of the following is NOT given as a reason for the end of Concorde operations?

    a. noise problems
    b. high running cost
    c. technical problems

2. According to Blake Scholl, what is the main improvement of the Overture aircraft over the Concorde?

    a. relaxed seating with more space between
    b. jet fuel that returns carbon to the atmosphere
    c. an aerodynamic shape to go through wind tunnels

3. What is the main objective of the development of the new supersonic plane?

    a. to show how much shorter air travel can be
    b. to allow people to spend less time travelling
    c. to offer a luxurious experience in the sky

 7 Retelling the Story ·······························

Re-tell the story presented in the video clip, including the following five keywords.

    the Concorde supersonic airplane   Overture Aircraft

    twice the speed of sound   sustainable aviation fuel

    100% carbon neutral

8 Your Opinion in Writing ···

Do you think new supersonic planes are the future of air travel? Why? Why not? Write your opinion.

_____

_____

_____

_____

_____

_____

9 ## Further Information ·· Audio 25

Read the passage below.

Sustainable Aviation Fuel: Safe, Reliable, Low Carbon

SAF is a biofuel used to power aircraft that has similar properties[*1] to conventional[*2] jet fuel but with a smaller carbon footprint[*3]. Depending on the feedstock[*4] and technologies used to produce it, SAF can reduce life cycle[*5] greenhouse gas emissions[*6]
5 dramatically compared to conventional jet fuel. Some emerging SAF pathways[*7] even have a net-negative[*8] greenhouse gas footprint.

Feedstocks suitable for SAF production:

 Oil seed plants and energy grasses [*9]

 Algae [*12]

 Municipal solid waste [*10]

 Fats, oils, and greases from cooking waste and meat production

 Agricultural and forestry residue [*11]

 Industrial carbon monoxide [*13] waste gas

Graphic by Emma Johnson, EESI

Notes

[*1] **property**「特性」／[*2] **conventional**「従来の」／[*3] **carbon footprint**「カーボン・フットプリント（炭素の足跡）」商品の循環過程を通して排出される温室効果ガスの排出量をCO_2に換算した指標。footprintは「（天然資源の）消費量」の意味。／[*4] **feedstock**「原料」／[*5] **life cycle**「製品の（製造から廃棄までの）循環過程」／[*6] **greenhouse gas emission**「温室効果ガス（の）排出」／[*7] **pathway**「可能性」／[*8] **net-negative**「正味（トータルでは）マイナス」／[*9] **energy grasses**「エネルギー源になる草・植物」／[*10] **municipal solid waste**「都市固形廃棄物（都市ごみ）」municipalは「地方自治体の（による）」／[*11] **agricultural and forestry residue**「農林廃棄物」／[*12] **algae**「藻（そう）類」／[*13] **carbon monoxide**「一酸化炭素」

Vocabulary Checklist

Check the boxes after reviewing the meanings
of the words listed below.

Unit 12
New Supersonic Plane

☐ marvel   ☐ costly

☐ be retired   ☐ aviation

☐ operational   ☐ atmosphere

☐ complaint   ☐ convert

☐ sustainable   ☐ ultimately

University Students Back 'Sleep Pods'

▶▶▶

マンチェスター大学の図書館では仮眠ポッドはおなじみの設備です。一部では無用の長物と見られていますが、実際に使われるようになっているのです。教育機関であれ職場であれ、睡眠不足は大きな問題です。仮眠ポッドは大成功をおさめ、導入を検討している企業もあります。仮眠の効用について考えてみましょう。

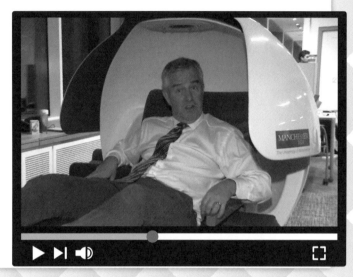

1 Video Watching for Gist

Watch the video and pick up five keywords. Guess what the main theme (topic/issue) of the video clip is.

2 Vocabulary Check – 1st Round

Match the following words and phrases with correct Japanese meanings.

1. self-conscious	・それだけの価値がある
2. drift off	・風変わりな
3. inaction	・人目を気にする
4. odd	・居眠りする
5. deserved	・活動しないこと

95

3 ▶ Video Watching & Script Reading 🔊 Audio 26

Watch the video and fill in the appropriate words in the blanks.

Reporter: In this 24-hour library at Manchester University, the nap pod is already a familiar feature. It promises comfort and escape at the touch of a few buttons, as librarian Mark Fossey explains.

5 **Mark Fossey:** It's really relaxing. It maybe seems like you would feel a bit self-conscious, but **1.**_____ **2.**_____ **3.**_____ you shut the lid and the music is surrounding you it's very easy to just drift off.

Reporter: Costing up to 10,000 pounds, the nap pod has been seen
10 by some as a white elephant. But it does **4.**_____ **5.**_____.

Student 1: Most people would just come back home and actually fall asleep for hours, whereas this one just makes you sleep 20 minutes and then you can go back, so I think
15 it's a really good idea and I see people using it.

Student 2: Facing deadlines, for example, I think it's a really good idea to be able to take a nap whenever you want.

Student 3: Some of us don't live that close to Uni, so then it's **6.**_____ **7.**_____ to have a place where you
20 can just take a nap.

Reporter: Now students at Edinburgh University fancy a slice of the inaction. Voting to get four nap pods to satisfy their demand for the odd forty winks.

Priyanka Radhakrishnan: There's two problems. There's sleep
25 deprivation, which I think anyone who has lived a student lifestyle knows that when you have **8.**_____ **9.**_____ **10.**_____, society is combined, trying to have a social life, and also completing assignments, sleep cannot be the priority for many

96

30   many students. That's something that we tried to tackle
        through napping.

Reporter: Sleeping on the job may not be every employer's idea of
        smart business, but the pods' makers say they help to
        boost productivity.

35 **Mike McCarthy:** So successful has the nap pod been, that some
        companies are considering introducing them in the
        workplace, so that stressed executives, or even reporters,
        can consider having a well-deserved break. This is Mike
        McCarthy for Sky News, unavailable for the next 20
40   minutes.

📖 **Notes**

***Title* Back** 「背中」のニュアンスは言葉遊びとして示されているだけで、ここでは「支持する」の意。
／***l*.1 Manchester University** イギリスはイングランド北西部にある大学。／***l*.2 nap** 「昼寝、うた
た寝」／***l*.2 pod** 「装置」／***l*.2 feature** 「（装置などの）機能」／***l*.10 white elephant** そのまま
訳すと白い象だが、「無用の長物」の意の慣用句として使われている。／***l*.10 does** 強調のために用
いている。／***l*.18 Uni** =University ／***l*.21 Edinburgh University** 英国、スコットランドの首都
エディンバラにある大学。／***l*.21 fancy** 「思い描く」／***l l*.21–22 a slice of the inaction** get a
slice of the action 「活動に参加する」をひねって inaction 「無活動（=昼寝）」を用いている。／***l*.23
forty winks** 「うたた寝、仮眠」／***l*.25 deprivation** 「不足、欠乏」／***l*.27 society** 課外活動など。
／***l*.35 So successful ... been** "The nap pod has been so successful" を倒置。

Vocabulary Check – 2nd Round

Choose the appropriate words below to fill in the blanks in the English sentences. Change forms if necessary.

| deadline | fancy | vote | lid | priority |

1. I _____ going for a walk in the park this evening.

2. He struggled to open the jar because the _____ was tightly sealed.

3. She worked diligently to meet the _____ for submitting her report.

4. Safety should always be the _____ when operating heavy machinery.

5. He was _____ best player in the American League.

True or False

Read the following statements and indicate whether they are true (T) or not (F) along with the reasons. If you cannot determine T or F from the text, indicate NG (not given).

1. The nap pod at Manchester University allows users to sleep for several hours.　　　　　　　　　　　　　　　**(T / F / NG)**

_____

2. The nap pods are primarily aimed at addressing sleep deprivation among students.　　　　　　　　　　　　　　　**(T / F / NG)**

_____

3. Public libraries are thinking of installing nap pods in some space.　**(T / F / NG)**

_____

Comprehension Check ·····································

Choose the best answer for each question.

1. What is the purpose of the nap pod at Manchester University?

   a. to reduce productivity among students

   b. to provide rest for students

   c. to address sleep deprivation in the community

2. What does the nap pod allow to do at workplace?

   a. It allows employees to sleep on the job.

   b. It provides a well-deserved break for executives.

   c. It helps to improve worker's productivity.

3. Which is mentioned as being considered for installation after votes in Edinburgh University?

   a. 24-hours library

   b. nap pods

   c. private study room

 # Retelling the Story ··

Re-tell the story presented in the video clip including the following five keywords.

| university | nap pod | student lifestyle | companies | workplace |

8 Your Opinion in Writing ·······································

Do you agree or disagree with the idea of installing nap pods in educational institutions? Why or why not?

9 **Further Information** ··· 🔊 Audio 27

Read the passage below.

Sleeping on the Job:
Customs from Countries around the World

China – Bring Your Bedroom to Work

In offices across China, due to longer working hours, many employers now advocate^{*1} a short nap after lunchtime to increase concentration. Certain offices have even installed temporary or permanent sleeping and washing facilities in their office spaces to

5 encourage employees to stay round the clock^{*2}.

Japan – Inemuri

Taking a nap at work could well be perceived as a sign of laziness^{*3}, but not in Japan. The hectic^{*4} lifestyle of Japan's city

10 dwellers has led to the wide-scale uptake of "inemuri", or "sleeping whilst present". Thanks to inemuri, Japanese workers can nap on public transport, at their desk or even during meetings – and it's commonly seen as a sign of hard work.

Spain – Siesta

15 Originating in Spain, the siesta is perhaps one of the most well-known daytime snoozing^{*5} traditions. This practice might be under threat, however, with new business laws introduced in 2016 limiting how late employees can work, and effectively reducing the time they have to squeeze^{*6} in an afternoon nap.

 Notes

> ^{*1} **advocate** 「推奨する」／^{*2} **round the clock** 「24時間体制で」／^{*3} **laziness** 「怠惰」／
> ^{*4} **hectic** 「非常に忙しい」／^{*5} **snooze** 「居眠りする、うたた寝する」／^{*6} **squeeze** 「～の時間を捻出する」

Vocabulary Checklist

Check the boxes after reviewing the meanings
of the words listed below.

Unit 13
University Students Back 'Sleep Pods'

☐ self-conscious   ☐ inaction

☐ lid   ☐ vote

☐ drift off   ☐ odd

☐ deadline   ☐ priority

☐ fancy   ☐ deserved

English Language Volunteer Teachers in Colorado Build Meaningful Connections for Immigrants

▶▶▶

コロラド州にあるインテルカンビオ・コミュニティセンターではマコーリーさんが移民の生徒たちに英語を教えています。地域のボランティアが移民に言葉を教えるのを支援するためのこのプログラムは、ボランティアの教師、そして生徒たちにとってどのような繋がりをもたらしているのでしょうか。

 ## Video Watching for Gist

Watch the video and pick up five keywords. Guess what the main theme (topic/issue) of the video clip is.

 ## Vocabulary Check – 1st Round

Match the following words and phrases with correct Japanese meanings.

1. run a fever	・〜向けに作られている
2. thermometer	・熱を出す
3. be geared towards	・体温計
4. be capable of	・適切な
5. relevant	・〜ができる、〜の能力がある

3 ▸ Video Watching & Script Reading 🔊 Audio 28

Watch the video and fill in the appropriate words in the blanks.

Reporter: At the Intercambio Community Center in Longmont, Colorado, Deepa McCauley is teaching immigrants how to talk about health in English.

Deepa McCauley: Running a fever doesn't mean that you're running.
5 Running a fever is, the temperature... Yes, exactly! The thermometer moves.

Reporter: McCauley's students come from around the globe. She doesn't have a teaching background but was trained by Intercambio. Executive director Lee Shainis says
10 the program is designed to help community volunteers teach language to immigrants.

Lee Shainis: We created our own training materials because we found that a lot of the materials 1._____ 2._____ were not directly geared towards volunteer teachers,
15 and we've had 5000 volunteer teachers since we started, you know, 18 years ago. And volunteers are capable of doing an amazing job, but they also need something 3._____ 4._____ 5._____, and also really practical and relevant.

20 **Deepa McCauley:** How's he feeling?

Class: Depressed.

Deepa McCauley: Oh, my child is depressed.

Student: From discrimination.

Deepa McCauley: Discrimination? Yep. Depression can come from
25 discrimination. My father, in India, he was an engineer. He came to America, he was collecting carts in the grocery store. He was depressed.

Student: Change in life.

Deepa McCauley: Big change in life.

30 **Lee Shainis:** Deepa is awesome. She was, you know, one of our many teachers who had zero experience as a volunteer teaching English when she first came in, and we've seen huge advancements in her quality of teaching and her quality of getting her students engaged.

35 **Deepa McCauley:** One of the main reasons I wanted to teach English is because my parents were first generation immigrants who didn't speak English and they had a really hard time and they wouldn't have had a **6.**_____ **7.**_____ if they had a place like Intercambio.

40 **Deepa McCauley:** This is a frown. So somebody says, I see your frown. This is... that, that right there, that's a frown. That's a frown.

Sylvia Gonzales Nava: My name is Sylvia Gonzales Nava. When I left my country, I didn't speak at all English. At all.

45 **Nava's grandson:** If my grandma only knew Spanish, I wouldn't know what she was saying.

Sylvia Gonzales Nava: That's why I speak English, because I want to have a good conversation with you.

Nava's grandson: Her English is getting better.

50 **Sylvia Gonzales Nava:** **8.**_____ **9.**_____ **10.**_____ .

Reporter: The volunteer teachers and their students both say the meaningful connections they have at their Intercambio classes build lasting community connections. For VOA News, I'm Shelley Schlender in Longmont, Colorado.

55 **Deepa McCauley:** You want to drink tea, right? Yeah. Green tea. You can drink green tea. Relax.

Notes

Title **Colorado** アメリカ西部にある州。南北にロッキー山脈が貫いており、全米で最も平均高度が高い州でもある。 *ℓ.1* **Intercambio** 「相互交流」スペイン語。／ *ℓ.40* **frown** [fraʊn] 「不機嫌な様子」ここでは「賛同しない」という意思を眉間にしわを寄せて示している。

Vocabulary Check – 2nd Round ⋯⋯⋯⋯⋯⋯

Choose the appropriate words below to fill in the blanks in the English sentences. Change forms if necessary.

| exactly | directly | advancement | discrimination | engage |

1. She worked hard and earned a promotion for her significant _____ of the company.

2. Please speak to the manager _____ if you have any concerns or questions.

3. That is _____ what I was hoping to find at the store.

4. We should work together to eliminate all forms of _____ and promote equality.

5. She _____ him in conversation because he had no acquaintances.

5 **True or False** ⋯⋯⋯⋯⋯⋯⋯⋯⋯⋯⋯⋯

Read the following statements and indicate whether they are true (T) or not (F) along with the reasons. If you cannot determine T or F from the text, indicate NG (not given).

1. Deepa McCauley has a professional teaching career. **(T / F / NG)**

_____

2. Intercambio Community Center provides training materials specifically designed for volunteer teachers. **(T / F / NG)**

_____

3. Nava's grandson has been studying Spanish at his school. **(T / F / NG)**

_____

106

6 Comprehension Check ·······································

Choose the best answer for each question.

1. What is the main focus of the Intercambio program?

    a. teaching volunteers how to collect grocery carts

    b. training immigrants to teach English

    c. helping volunteers teach language to immigrants

2. Why did Deepa McCauley decide to teach English?

    a. because she wanted to be a teacher from her childhood

    b. because she had prior teaching experience

    c. because her parents struggled a lot

3. What is the impact of Intercambio classes on community connections?

    a. They result in temporary connections.

    b. They have had short-term connections.

    c. They build lasting community connections.

7 Retelling the Story ·······································

Re-tell the story presented in the video clip, including the following five keywords.

| teaching | volunteer teacher | practical | program | connection |

_____

_____

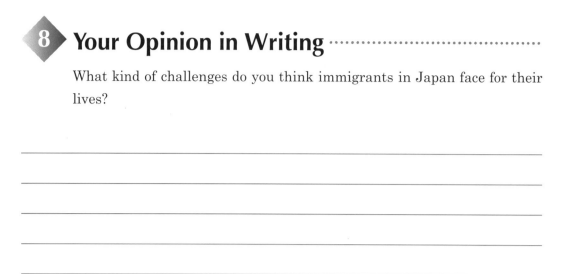

8 ▸ Your Opinion in Writing ···

What kind of challenges do you think immigrants in Japan face for their lives?

9 ▶ **Further Information** ·································· 🔊 Audio 29

Read the passage below.

Japan to Double*¹ Language Support Budget
for Foreign Children

The government will strengthen support for foreign children in need of Japanese-language education with a planned doubling of the budget as part of efforts to ensure they are not missing out on learning opportunities, the education ministry*² said.

5　Based on a survey conducted last year, the ministry estimates that more than 19,000 out of the around 124,000 foreign children of elementary or junior high school-age in Japan do not attend school at all, including international schools.

In accounting for the lack of attendance, the ministry said some
10　children and guardians*³ may not possess*⁴ sufficient command*⁵ of the Japanese language and support also varies among local governments, with many only sending notices regarding enrollment in Japanese.

The ministry allocated a budget of around 700 million yen ($6.6
15　million) this fiscal year for support measures, which included covering one-third of the labor costs of Japanese-language tutors and assistants to provide advice in children's native tongues.

The ministry plans to request a doubling of the budget for fiscal 2021 to meet the growing needs of local governments. It will also
20　create multilingual video materials and hold training sessions for teachers at public schools to enable the admission of more foreign children.

 Notes

*¹ **Japan to double** 名詞＋to不定詞で、名詞＋will＋動詞の意味を表す新聞の見出し独特の用法。double は新聞の見出しでは「倍増する」という意味の動詞で使われることも多い。*² **education ministry** 「文部科学省」／*³ **guardian** 「保護者」／*⁴ **possess** 「（能力などを）有する」／*⁵ **command** 「運用能力」

Vocabulary Checklist

Check the boxes after reviewing the meanings
of the words listed below.

Unit 14
English Language Volunteer Teachers in Colorado Build Meaningful Connections for Immigrants

☐ run a fever

☐ exactly

☐ thermometer

☐ directly

☐ be geared to [towards]

☐ be capable of

☐ relevant

☐ discrimination

☐ advancement

☐ engage

Melting of Kashmir Glaciers Causes Concern About Water Shortages

▶▶▶

日本でも年々酷暑が深刻化し、みなさんの中にも温暖化に対して危機感を持っている方もいるのではないでしょうか。インドとパキスタン支配下のカシミール地方でも氷河が溶けつつあります。もはやこの現象を対岸の火事として考えることはできないでしょう。

 ## Video Watching for Gist

Watch the video and pick up five keywords. Guess what the main theme (topic/issue) of the video clip is.

 ## Vocabulary Check – 1st Round

Match the following words and phrases with correct Japanese meanings.

1. vanish	・紛争
2. conflict	・残量
3. reserve	・倫理的な
4. impact	・消滅する
5. ethical	・〜に影響を与える

3 ▸ Video Watching & Script Reading 🔊 Audio 30

Watch the video and fill in the appropriate words in the blanks.

Reporter: Six glaciers in the Himalayas have nearly vanished since 1980, according to satellite data mapping. And researchers say hundreds of glaciers in the region are melting, all **1.**_____ **2.**_____ the impact of a warming planet.

Shakil Ahmad Romshoo: Every year you go to a glacier, we are seeing on an average almost a meter of thickness decrease in the glaciers. So that gives you **3.**_____ **4.**_____ about the state and the status of the glacier melting in Jammu Kashmir.

Reporter: In the Himalayan region, over 14,000 small and large alpine glaciers have been identified, including those in India and Pakistan-controlled Kashmir. Some of the region's biggest glaciers can be found in areas between North-Eastern India and Afghanistan.

Dr. Govind Singh: We are seeing glaciers melt very fast and the way they melt is such that we can't estimate how long they will last. We can't guess how much water will flow into our rivers in the next 5 to 20 years. So if this continues, I can see conflicts and disputes in the future between Pakistan and India over water shortages.

Reporter: Shifts in ice and glacier reserves have already **5.**_____ **6.**_____ **7.**_____ on agriculture. Farmers in Indian-administered Kashmir

25   are turning paddy fields into apple orchards.

Shabir Ahmed: There is a problem of water in the land. The crop is not growing properly. Pollution has increased. There was snow on the mountains. It was slowly melting. The annual paddy crop suffered a loss of 50%.

30 **Reporter:** Local agriculture sustains the bulk of India's and Pakistan's populations, and the two nations have a long history of disagreements over water management. Those disagreements, experts say, will intensify as the glaciers disappear.

35 **Dr. Govind Singh:** If the two countries don't stop fighting, 8._____ 9._____ 10._____ the disputes increase, as we can already foresee, but also our two nations' water sustainability will also be impacted. I think we've reached the very interesting point here that

40   not only do the two countries need to stop fighting for ethical and human rights reasons, but also because of environmental reasons.

Reporter: And South Asia is particularly vulnerable to climate change. Over the next 30 years, if nothing is done,

45   researchers predict water shortages, drought and rising sea levels could create some 60 million climate refugees in South Asia. For Zubair Dar in Srinagar, Kashmir, Bezhan Hamdard, VOA News.

Notes

Title **glacier**「氷河」／*ℓ.2* **satellite**「衛星」／*ℓ.2* **data** 本文では「ダータ」[dáːtə] と発音されている。data は「データ」[deɪtə] と発音される場合もある。／*ℓ.7* **decrease** 正しくは decreases。／*ℓ.9* **status**「状況」／*ℓ.10* **Jammu Kashmir**「ジャンムー・カシミール州」インド、パキスタン北部の国境地域。領有を巡っては印パ戦争など大小の軍事衝突が絶えない。／*ℓ.12* **alpine**「高山の」／*ℓ.13* **Pakistan-controlled Kashmir**「パキスタンが実効支配しているカシミール地域」／*ℓ.20* **dispute**「論争」／*ℓ.22* **shift**「変化」／*ℓ.24* **Indian-administered**「インド統治下の」／*ℓ.25* **paddy field**「水田」／*ℓ.25* **orchard**「果樹園」／*ℓ.30* **bulk of ~**「~の大部分」／*ℓ.40* **not only do the two countries need to stop …** この do は強調を表す助動詞。／*ℓ.46* **climate refugee**「気候変動避難民」気候変動や、それによる災害で避難を余儀なくされた人々。

4 ▸ Vocabulary Check – 2nd Round ·····················

Choose the appropriate words below to fill in the blanks in the English sentences. Change forms if necessary.

| foresee | identify | intensify | sustain | vulnerable |

1. Babies need lots of care because they are extremely _____ to infections.

2. The alert level was raised as the storm _____.

3. Scientists _____ humans living on Mars within the next 200 years.

4. Economic growth cannot _____ without a rise in inflation.

5. After years of research, scientists _____ the virus that causes the disease.

5 ▸ True or False ··

Read the following statements and indicate whether they are true (T) or not (F) along with the reasons. If you cannot determine T or F from the text, indicate NG (not given).

1. The Himalayan glaciers are getting thinner by around one meter each year.

(T / F / NG)

_____

2. People in the Himalayan region are worried that rivers will flood as the glaciers melt fast.

(T / F / NG)

_____

3. Water shortage can lead to further conflict between nations.

(T / F / NG)

_____

6 ▶ Comprehension Check ·····································

Choose the best answer for each question.

1. What can we learn from satellite data mapping?

   a. geographical changes in the Himalayan mountains

   b. impact of global warming on glaciers in the Himalayas

   c. decreasing paddy fields and increasing orchards

2. Why is the Kashmir region important to the people of India and Pakistan?

   a. because it is a rich agricultural area that feeds them

   b. because it is less affected by pollution from the cities

   c. because it has a long history of managing water from glaciers

3. If no action is taken against climate change in the coming decades, what will happen to the people in South Asia?

   a. The type of food grown may change.

   b. Pollution may affect their health.

   c. The number of refugees may increase.

7 ▶ Retelling the Story ·····································

Re-tell the story presented in the video clip, including the following five keywords.

hundreds of glaciers in the Himalayas	water management

impact on agriculture	disputes	be vulnerable to climate change

Your Opinion in Writing ·······························

How do you relate the water problems of the people in Jammu Kashmir to your own? Write your opinion.

_____

_____

_____

_____

_____

_____

9 Further Information ································· 🔊 Audio 31

Read the passage below.

Water Inequality is a Global Issue

Water is not a developing-world problem. It's an everyone, everywhere problem. And it's one of the most pressing issues of our time. We all need and rely on it, and as competition for water escalates around the world, the strain[*1] of growing populations,

5 climate change and political tensions add even more pressure to ensuring we all have access.

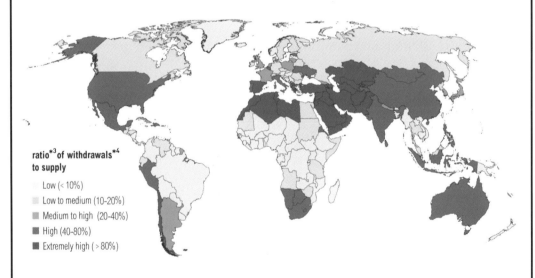

Water Stress[*2] by Country: 2040

ratio[*3] of withdrawals[*4]
to supply

Low (< 10%)
Low to medium (10-20%)
Medium to high (20-40%)
High (40-80%)
Extremely high (> 80%)

NOTE: Projections are based on a business-as-usual scenario using SSP2 and RCP8.5.

For more: ow.ly/RiWop

 WORLD RESOURCES INSTITUTE

We don't have long before our
options begin to dry up Image
© World Resources Institute

 Notes

[*1] **strain** 「試練」／ [*2] **water stress** 「水ストレス、水不足」淡水資源量に占める淡水採取量の割合。数値が高いほど水不足の状態を表す。／ [*3] **ratio** 「割合」／ [*4] **(water) withdrawal** 「取水量」河川などから水を取り入れること。

Vocabulary Checklist

Check the boxes after reviewing the meanings
of the words listed below.

Unit 15
Melting of Kashmir Glaciers Causes Concern
About Water Shortages

☐ vanish

☐ impact

☐ identify

☐ conflict

☐ reserve

☐ be sustained

☐ intensify

☐ foresee

☐ ethical

☐ vulnerable